What's in Your House to Avoid DEBT Traps?

What's in Your House to Avoid DEBT Traps?

Ramona Patterson

Scripture taken from the New King James Version®
Copyright© 1982 by Thomas Nelson, Inc.
Used by permission. All rights reserved.

Scripture quotations from the Amplified® Bible,
Copyright © 1954, 1958, 1962, 1964, 1965, 1987
 by The Lockman Foundation
Used by permission. (www.Lockman.org (http://www.Lockman.org)

Scripture quotations from *THE MESSAGE*. Copyright ©
by Eugene H. Peterson 1993, 1994, 1995, 1996, 2000, 2001, 2002.
Used by permission of NavPress Publishing Group.

Salvation Prayer:
Used by permission of Dr. Bill Winston, Senior Pastor,
Living Word Christian Center
Forest Park, IL

What's in Your House to Avoid Debt Traps?
ISBN # 978-0-615-74917-4

Blesspatt Books
338 South Sharon Amity #140
Charlotte, NC 28211

Published in the USA

This book is dedicated in loving memory of my dad, Robert A. Clark Sr., whose love, guidance, fiscal integrity and sound money management skills have been a constant source of inspiration.

Acknowledgements

To my mother, Marjorie Clark, and my daughter, Lauren Rashaan: Words cannot express my gratitude for all of your faithful support and priceless encouragement. I love you dearly and appreciate your always being there.

To Pastor Robyn Gool and his wife, Marilyn: My sincerest thanks for your excellent leadership and keen perception in discerning God's voice and teaching me how to follow Him.

Table of Contents

Introduction

Once the reality sets in that you're head over heels in debt, don't panic. Tossing fear into the equation would only help wipe you out. Believe it or not, God has a plan for turning what looks like a hopeless situation around. When we seek His help, He answers, usually not in an audible voice and maybe not with a three-step plan. But if you're willing to try something new, He's got the perfect plan for bringing you out of debt forever. This book explores a variety of debt-tackling solutions, as well as traps set by our trillion-dollar financial industry to keep us in debt and hustling backward.

When God sent the Prophet Jeremiah to warn the Israelites that serving pagan gods would only lead to their destruction, they didn't believe him. The prophet urged them to return to God or become brutally enslaved by foreigners. Jeremiah did his best to convince them to choose God's abundant life. But they refused to listen. The only way to avoid the perils of slavery and thrive as a nation was for them to renew their relationships with God and seek His advice. Likewise, He wants to reveal His plan to us, cause us to rise above oppression and break debt's deadly grip over our spirits, minds and finances. Notice the prophet's instructions to the Israelites in Jeremiah 33:3 (AMP).

"Call to Me and I will answer you and show you great and mighty things, fenced in and hidden, which you do not know (do not distinguish and recognize, have knowledge of and understand)."

God's plan has always been to prosper His children. That's especially relevant now since we're living in the final phase of the last dispensation of grace before Christ returns. During this short timeframe, He has promised to multiply our wealth so we can live victoriously and radically finance the gospel. But unfortunately, believers are as weighed down with debt as unbelievers. Debt has caused the wealth God promised us through His covenant with Abraham to instead evade us.

Yet, God's plan for us hasn't changed. He wants to give us new wealth-building strategies. But as long as you're consumed with just staying above water, you'll fear trying new approaches. Once you commit in your heart to come out of debt, the strategy to accomplish your goal will become clear. Throughout the Old Testament, God revealed His plans to those who sought His guidance through the prophets. Although He still speaks through modern-day prophets, He expects us to rely more on the Bible (His word) and His promptings in our spirits. By applying spiritual wisdom and practical knowledge, we're taking a step of faith toward financial freedom.

So take a deep breath, exhale and decide no matter how long it takes, you're going to apply some of the debt-reduction strategies you learn from this book, and you're coming out of debt. You must be determined to keep plowing forward, knowing your faith in God will cause you to succeed, and He will give you all the insight and understanding you need.

Debt: An Age-old trap

Thousands of years ago when the Israelites borrowed money, lenders trying to get richer quicker added exorbitant amounts of interest and fees to their debts. Although our legislators have spent billions of taxpayer dollars to "regulate" America's financial industry, nothing much has changed, except today's system is far more corrupt.

During the Roman Empire, people recognized the system's corruption, but could do little about it under dictatorships. Today, the public is just gullible and misinformed. They assume their money is protected by the government. Yet, nothing could be further from the truth. While many realize it shouldn't take 20 years to pay back a $3,000 debt, not many pay attention to sophisticated debt traps, or the seemingly harmless mounds of quicksand sucking them deeper into this ruthless cycle. They assume any shady dealings would trigger the watchdogs overseeing the federal government's arsenal of fair lending laws to "sick 'em."

But not so! While the American public snores, special interest groups continue gaining control of the nation's purse strings. Until something blows up, elected officials pretend not to notice all the palms being greased. Just like wolves, who know to start off garnishing only a few chickens at a time, they realize hardly anyone suspects mega-mess deals like Merrill Lynch and Fannie Mae until it's too late. By then, the money's been stolen and spent and the public's got to pay for it.

Chapter 1
Stop Borrowing

"STOP BORROWING?" That's a lot easier said than done, right? But avoiding debt's not hard. I once heard someone say, "You don't have to be a financial genius to come out of debt. You simply have to hate it." My hatred of debt dates back to childhood. I grew up in a middle-class family with two brothers, who were pretty smart in math. But when it came to spending, I was much more conservative. I'm not sure if it had to do with one being six years older than me and the other, six years younger, or the fact I was so "math stupid" I thought spending less would leave me less to keep up with.

When we were young, my dad was a public school math teacher and my mom worked in accounting. My mom paid the electric bill, bought our clothes and paid our allowances. My dad paid for everything else, including the groceries. Provided my brothers and I completed our Saturday chores to my mom's satisfaction, she gave us allowances twice a month when she got paid. I was in sixth grade when I began earning my $25 allowance.

Out of it I bought jeans and jewelry; paid for lunch at school; bought the latest albums and paid for movies, concerts and other special outings with my friends. I also set aside a small savings, which I tapped into to buy Christmas and birthday presents. My parents strictly upheld the one house rule regarding allowances, which was: Once your money was gone, it was gone. They didn't seem to care if you lost it, squandered it or gave it all away. The point was they weren't replacing it. They felt since they didn't have the option of running back to their employers between paydays and requesting an advance, they weren't giving us that option. Besides, they were old school. They felt replacing money we had blown would be rewarding us for poorly managing money.

By the time I reached high school, my mom had increased my allowance to reflect her pay raises. But as my social activities increased, I was often penniless by the time my next allowance rolled around. Even when I offered what I thought were some pretty darn good excuses to justify them giving me a little advance – pitched in on a school project, gave money to a homeless person, or made a small loan to my brothers – they didn't budge, but insisted I learn to prioritize my spending.

When I learned my favorite cousin had been approved for her first credit card, I thought a credit card would certainly help me prioritize my spending. She told me how convenient it was and easy to obtain. Although she was only a few months older than me, I had always admired her keen street sense. I attributed her clever wits to having grown up in a single-parent household in one of Norfolk's largest and toughest public housing projects. It wasn't until years later, I realized street wits and business sense are two totally different things. She thought I would be a prime candidate for a credit card since I now had a part-time summer job and was earning my own money. I agreed since I couldn't remember my parents ever running into problems managing their credit cards.

I was 16 when I applied for my first credit card, and surprisingly, got it. Unlike my cousin's card, which contained only one ladies' store, mine authorized charges of up to $200 at four different stores in Portsmouth's Tower Mall. One was my favorite shoe store, along with three department stores. A little gun shy of credit, I got in the habit of charging only one item at a time and paying it off before charging anything else. Except at Christmas time, my balance rarely exceeded $30, which was pretty affordable on my allowance once my summer job ended.

Assuming my cousin was much more knowledgeable about how credit worked than I, I had no qualms about allowing her to charge a $75 pair of designer sandals on my shoe store account. I didn't think it would be a problem, especially since she promised to pay it off as soon as her financial aid check arrived in about a month. But by the time it arrived, she had run up other bills and was doling out excuses for why she needed more time to pay. Finally, my sophomore year in college, she gave me the $75, but not one dime of the interest and late fees I had paid. It was a sobering lesson learned the hard way, but a valuable lesson on careless attitudes toward debt.

Here's how Moses warned Israel not to borrow:

"The Lord will open to you His good treasure, the heavens, to give the rain to your land in its season, and to bless all the work of your hand. You shall lend to many nations, but you shall not borrow." -- Deuteronomy 28:12 (New Kings James)

A Portrait of the World's Financial System

Some of the most insightful revelation of how the world's debt-ridden financial system operates is visible in the 30th Chapter of Genesis. This astonishing parallel begins to unfold in verses 34 and 35 as Jacob recommends his wages to his boss, Laban. Laban anxiously agreed to his proposal, authorizing Jacob to keep only the blemished flocks – the streaked, speckled and spotted sheep and goats, along with the black sheep as his income. In other words, the two men agreed that Jacob would surrender all of the perfect, unblemished animals to his boss and keep for himself the ones marred by discoloration. But that same day, Laban broke their verbal agreement by stealing all of the streaked, speckled and spotted flocks and giving them to his sons (Genesis 30:34-35).

That's a splitting image of today's financial system laced with convoluted contracts and good-faith promises designed to prevent consumers from understanding exactly how money transactions work. But sadly, before the ink on the paper dries, corporations, just like greedy Laban, have in place strategies to sift away as much of your money as they can in profits, while cutting back on the services and benefits they promise you. Later, this chapter confirms there's no reason to try to beat or fix the system. It may have been just as easy for Jacob to steal the flocks back. But instead of lowering himself to Laban's level, Jacob, a natural-born descendent of Abraham, relied on God's covenant with Abraham for a plan.

The covenant obligated God to bless Abraham and his seed forever. As believers we are the spiritual seed of Abraham and heirs with Christ to everything God owns. Shouldn't we rely on God's promises to us, rather than on people and circumstances?

When faced with adversity, we simply have to humble ourselves and trust God as we walk in the integrity of His love. And He will give us a strategy to excel that will exceed all expectations. While Jacob realized his employer was a wretched scoundrel, he didn't waste any time trying to discredit Laban or expose his horrible reputation. Instead, Jacob focused his attention on getting God's strategy and working it.

Here's the simple, but clever strategy Jacob worked: He peeled white strips in the rods of trees, placed them in the watering troughs so his strong flocks coming to drink would be forced to focus only on the speckled, spotted and streaked images they saw. That way, when they conceived, they would only reproduce images of what they saw (verses 37-39). The plan worked perfectly. Jacob wound up with all the strong dual-colored flocks and black sheep, and Laban got the perfect looking, but sickly and weak solid colored animals. The outcome of the story was Jacob became exceedingly rich with tons of flocks, servants, camels and donkeys.

Isn't it amazing Jacob was able to determine the appearance of his flocks' offspring by simply controlling their focal points? To do so, Jacob had to have already focused his energies on what he valued most – achieving financial success for his family. Just as interesting was the fact he only worked his plan among strong flocks and left feeble ones alone to default to Laban.

Whenever I've gotten down in the dumps, my mind was consumed replaying negative thoughts. The more I concentrated on them, the worse it got. When we focus our attention on feeble flocks – roadblocks set by others, money shortages and the dismal economic outlook and criminal activity broadcasted as news, those images zap our energy and diminish our joy, peace and motivation to excel. If we're not careful, before long, we become content with just surviving.

Understanding Collections

The corporate debt collection system operates a lot like Laban too. It not only pits collectors against consumers, but creates a vicious cut-throat environment internally as employees relentlessly vie for the same pot of commission money, not realizing the number of winners is always predetermined. Just like with the lottery, not everyone can hit.

When I started in Corporate Communications at a bank, I knew little about the business. I was hired by senior management to create communication strategies that were credible enough to boost sales and eliminate suspicions of their motives. My job was convincing sales people that every new product, policy and procedure was designed to help them earn more money, whether true or false. Since I rarely interacted directly with them and knew little about how changes affected their pockets, I assumed greed was causing highly paid sales execs to be disgruntled and suspicious of changes. Even though some of our top-performing millionaires were suing the company, I refused to believe the company, which was rewarding me so generously, was deliberately reducing payouts to its sales force. I was what you'd call "densely naïve."

But after being laid off in a major bank merger, I landed on the low end of the totem pole in collections with the nation's largest auto financier. That's where my rose-colored glasses fell off. Just a few months into the new job, I realized the bank's sales teams weren't paranoid after all. But like commissioned bill collectors, they had to fight like crazy to prevent senior management from stealing their bonuses.

Month end is the most critical period for sales execs and collectors on commission because it's the deadline for reaching monthly performance goals. Where they stand the last day of the month determines whether or not they receive bonuses and if so, how much. That's when they're forced to turn up the heat, using all kinds of tactics to pistol whip you into paying. For the most part, their harsh speech shouldn't be taken personally. They're under tremendous pressure to reach performance goals, pay their own bills and prevent the company from stealing their bonuses. So unless you're ready to pay on the spot or commit to a set payment arrangement, there's no use in answering most collections calls.

If you've ever been harassed by automated phone dialers, realize past-due customers aren't the only ones being pulverized by these monsters. Companies routinely misuse automated call routing systems to eliminate commissions. If you've setup an arrangement to pay two weeks from now, and the automated dialer calls you every day, it's wasting time your account manager needs to reach other customers. Likewise, collectors who were consistently routed paying customers with high auto loan balances ($20,000 to $50,000) could quickly reach their goals and with little effort. But those routed callers with tiny balances (under $5,000) could resolve five times as many accounts and never hit the goal, which meant they wouldn't qualify for a bonus. On top of that, they faced disciplinary action for consistently missing goals.

To prevent the corporate office from raising quotas, our collections center would stall on processing accounts, pretending paperwork never arrived, which forced customers to send the same documents over and over.

To ensure account executives reached revenue goals on the branch level where I sold mortgages and personal loans, we were required to process customers' postdated checks ahead of time without their authorization. The rationale was most banks close at 5 p.m. on Fridays and wouldn't be able to post payments until the following week. Unfortunately, this led to a lot of bounced checks and furious customers.

Just think if companies use such unethical tactics with those on their payrolls, how trustworthy are they with your money?

Chapter 2
Understand Consolidations

Consolidation Loans

When you're juggling more bills than you've got cash to cover, it's possible a consolidation loan may offer you some relief. The objective of any consolidation should be to compress your debts, give you more breathing room and save you money. If you're considering options that don't entail all three, you're likely barking up the wrong tree. Even though past-due bills can make anyone a little antsy, the last thing you want to do is jump out of the boat and into a consolidated whale's belly.

The most effective consolidations are those you initiate on your own, using your own savings or extra cash. But if you don't have enough ready reserves to meet your monthly obligations, you might consider talking to reputable debt consolidation agencies, credit unions or banks. Notice finance companies are not included in this list. The reason is they profit most from your dilemma by charging you exorbitant interest and fees.

This is how a consolidation loan works: A lender loans you enough money to pay off all or a portion of your creditors. Some lenders give customers payoff checks already addressed to each creditor for the account balance. Some lenders go a step further and mail payoff checks to their clients' creditors. Whether you're using the loan to pay off 20 debts or just two, the consolidation combines your debts, leaving you with one bill – the consolidation loan.

For those who are seriously over-extended, but willing to sacrifice to pay off bills, non-profit credit counselors and debt consolidation agencies generally place you in a better position to come out of debt and manage your own finances. Such agencies charge pennies on a dollar to manage your accounts, renegotiate your terms, consolidate your debt and send payments to your creditors. They do everything except earn the money for you.

They contact each creditor and negotiate with them to cut your interest rates and payments in half, so you can afford them. But most debt-laden consumers ignorantly avoid these agencies, which are especially designed to help them. Somehow, big financial institutions have convinced the public that using these agencies would cause the words "credit counseling" to appear on their credit reports, which in turn, would ruin their credit ratings. It's simply not true.

Although credit counseling would be noted on your credit report, it would not hurt your credit rating. Besides, nothing hurts your credit more than late payments and nonpayment. Folks with stellar credit generally don't consolidate their bills unless their income has been significantly reduced or they find lower money-saving interest rates. The fact of the matter is coming out of debt is 10 times more advantageous than building a credit report. Eliminating bills always improves your credit rating when you're over extended.

But before sashaying into the nearest financial center to ask the first warm body to pay off your debts, make sure you're at least familiar with your own financial dilemma. Otherwise you're as docile as a dazed doe, a sitting duck, waiting to be pierced by the first buckshot. Why? Because you haven't taken time to request and review your own credit report. By law you're entitled to receive one free copy from each of the three major credit reporting agencies every year. But if you never request them, guess what? You'll never receive them, and you'll be at the mercy of credit companies to disclose to you the content of your report. Since you haven't bothered to look at it, they can tell you whatever they want. Unfortunately, they also base your interest rate on what's reflected in your credit report. Your overall ranking, number of creditors, account balances, number of delinquencies, income-to-debt ratio and whether or not you own a home are all factored into the equation.

Your credit report arms you with the in-depth research needed to intelligently discuss your financial history with creditors. Only you can determine if it contains errors, such as judgments and settlements that have already been resolved, or if it reflects mistaken identity. Also, a quick glance over your credit report would allow you to identify any fraudulent transactions.

You may have been denied financing on a new car or house because your credit report shows you're late paying on an Oklahoma cattle ranch and your yacht in Boca Raton was repossessed. You can argue all day long that you've never owned either of those, but unless you contest it through the credit bureaus, no legitimate lender is going to take your word. Until you correct it, it is what it is. So why leave home to go talk with complete strangers about your finances before taking time to assess what you owe and who you owe?

Ignorance puts you at a serious disadvantage. It's got to be humiliating sitting across the desk as a 24-year-old loan officer rambles on about your mortgage being two months past due and your last car being repossessed. All this time, you thought your auto financier had exonerated you for the four missed car payments, especially since you'd been religiously making your payments ahead of time for the past three years.

I was amazed when I sat across the desk from fairly sophisticated-looking consumers who didn't have a clue about who they owed, not to mention how much they owed them. They would say things like, "I thought I paid that off," or "I disputed that charge three years ago. That shouldn't still be on my credit report."

It's your job as a consumer to make sure your credit report is accurate, not the folks working at the credit bureaus. Legally, credit bureaus may show your undisputed late payments for seven years, but they can show bankruptcies and judgments for more than 10 years.

Avoiding the traps

Just as ridiculous to me are consumers who rely on their finance companies to decide which creditors they should pay off. When I worked for a Fortune 500 finance company, the number of customers who simply trusted me to choose their accounts to consolidate surprised me. They automatically assumed they could trust me to look out for their best interest even when faced with the decision of whether to put theirs or the company's interest first. You should never blindly trust outsiders with your finances even if you've done business with a company for 20 years. Loan officers are paid to get as much money out of you as they possibly can. Their primary focus is the company's bottom line and how much they can earn in commission.

Regardless of what companies tell you, the customers' problems or objectives are always secondary in the lending industry. The company's profits are always first. But when you don't know who you owe or what you owe, chances are slim you'll know which of your creditors offer the best interest rates. In order for you to benefit from a consolidation loan, you must make sure the new rate you're being offered is lower than the rate you had.

Pay close attention to the terms of a consolidation loan. Often times, the rate offered will be lower than some of your existing rates, but higher than others. When consolidating, you should concentrate on paying off your most costly debts first – those with higher interest rates. But if you're not careful, you could walk away with a mere "convenience consolidation" in which the lender has given you a lower easy-to-manage payment, but is charging you substantially more interest on the money you borrowed.

If you're not on top of the game, you can easily get hustled into taking a consolidation loan that's more harmful than helpful. Here's how it works. The loan officer reviews the customer's credit report and lists all the creditors and interest rates charged on each account. The lender leads customers to believe that when all the interest percentages are tallied up, they're spending substantially more than they would if their bills were consolidated. The truth is there's no reason to tally up interest percentages, except to distort the picture.

Each interest charge is applied separately to only a portion of the borrower's total debt. The conversation between the customer and loan officer would go something like this:

Loan officer: "Mr. Smith, you've got $20,000 in debts. I see almost all your money is going toward interest."

Mr. Smith: "That's why I'm trying to pay everybody off just as quickly as I can."

Loan officer: "You're paying 10 percent on your car note, 21 percent on your Sears account, 17 percent to Penney's, 4 percent to Sallie Mae, 5 percent to Freddie Mac, 6 percent to Direct Student Loans and 16 percent to Citibank. When you add it all up, that's 79 percent just in interest. Let me pay off all those bills for you with a consolidation loan. Instead of paying all that interest to all those different creditors, you'll just have one payment and one interest rate, which means you won't be paying out nearly as much each month."

Mr. Smith: "What's your rate?"

Loan officer: "18 percent."

Mr. Smith: "Wow! That's pretty high."

Loan officer: "But we're helping you to keep money in your pocket by giving you one low payment with a fixed rate. You won't have to worry about keeping up with payments to all those creditors each month."

Because it sounds like a great deal, many customers get hustled into consolidating, not realizing they've just been sold on a comparison between apples and Snicker bars. Although one has nothing to do with the other, a skilled salesperson can easily weave a sales pitch around totally unrelated factors without blinking. As long as it sounds good and is delivered with a hint of sincerity, your average Joe Blow assumes it must be in his best interest.

As a rule of thumb, when you're offered a lower rate, it's generally in your best interest to consolidate high-interest loans. But rarely is there a practical reason to consolidate low-interest accounts into loans with higher interest rates.

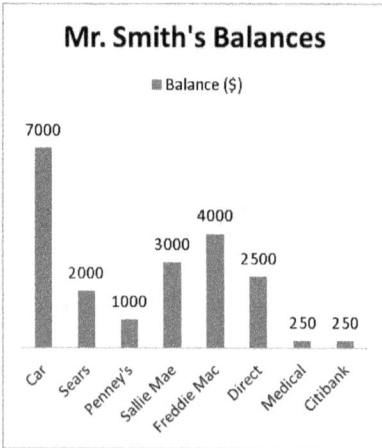

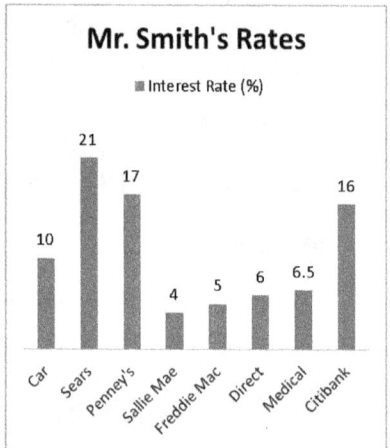

Mr. Smith's Balances

■ Balance ($)

Car	Sears	Penney's	Sallie Mae	Freddie Mac	Direct	Medical	Citibank
7000	2000	1000	3000	4000	2500	250	250

Mr. Smith's Rates

■ Interest Rate (%)

Car	Sears	Penney's	Sallie Mae	Freddie Mac	Direct	Medical	Citibank
10	21	17	4	5	6	6.5	16

Mr. Smith's Debts

	Car	Sears	Penney's	Sallie Mae	Freddie Mac	Direct	Medical	Citibank
Balance ($1,000s)	7	2	1	3	4	2.5	0.25	0.25
Interest Rate (%)	10	21	17	4	5	6	6.5	16

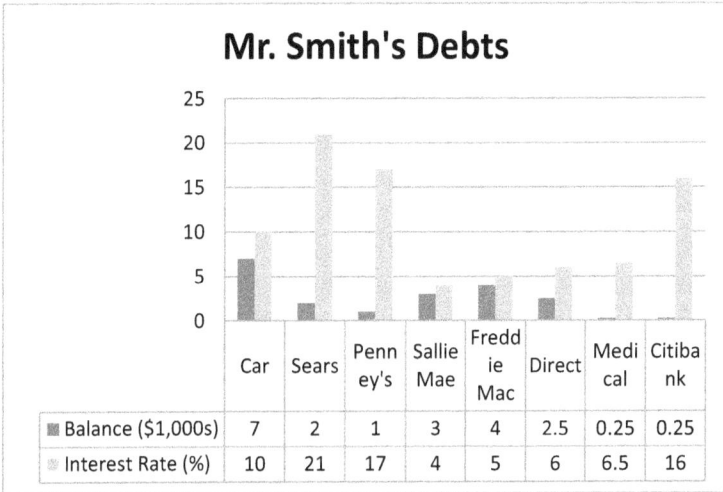

If Mr. Smith agrees to consolidate his bills, it will cost him a lot more than he bargained for. The interest rate on his $7,000 car note balance would jump from 10 percent to 18 percent.

Interest charges on his $3,000 Sallie Mae balance would jump from 4 to 18 percent. His Freddie Mac and Direct Student Loan accounts financed at 4 percent and 5 percent would jump to 18 percent. The only account that he could refinance without losing a lot of money would be his Sears account currently financed at 21 percent. Even if the finance company offered Mr. Smith a 6 percent rate to refinance just the two $250 Citibank and medical account balances, which, let's say he has been paying for years, he might save more money if he declined the offer and used his own cash to pay extra on the two accounts.

Because he's near the end of these two loans, almost all of his monthly payment goes to principal. A refinance would reverse that, causing about 98 percent of his new payment to go to interest. For this reason, it is rarely in a customer's best interest to refinance a loan just to bring an account current. Pushing late payments to the end of a loan will simply cause you to pay twice as much or more in interest, which does not benefit you. Collectors make this offer to delinquent customers just to get them off their books, so they can achieve their commission goals. An amendment or modification to lower your rate would lower your payment and save you much more money. But we'll discuss that in detail a little later.

As unethical as it may seem, many finance companies won't think twice about refinancing your student loans that carry annual rates of two to four percent with consolidation loans financed at rates exceeding 18 percent. To accept such an agreement is being penny-wise and pound-foolish. Therefore, you may wind up paying as much as five times more than you should. That's because you never took the time to review your credit report or bill statements to determine your interest rates and credit worthiness beforehand. Failing to carefully consider your options before engaging predators in your finances can be costly.

"That's ludicrous," you might say. But that's happening every day all over the country. Many major financial institutions have policies that encourage loan officers not to refinance low-interest government subsidized loans. In many cases, they're merely tongue-in-cheek best practices. Since there is no penalty for employees who violate these policies, this leaves consumers at the mercy of loan officers. It basically boils down to whether the banker you're dealing with has a conscience or not. Lending institutions are well aware of their inability to compete with low-interest government-backed loans. But most aren't willing to forego a loan to protect you from paying 10 times more in interest. After all, interest is their bread and butter.

One day, an elderly woman came into our finance office to borrow $10,000 to pay off her husband's medical bills. To qualify her for a personal loan, I had to consolidate some of the small bills that showed up on her credit report. Otherwise, she wouldn't have met the income-to-debt ratio (approximately a 35 percent margin) requirement. She had an excellent credit rating and payment history. Her credit report reflected several student loans, which were being consistently paid by her three well-educated, gainfully employed children.

As I verified her creditors and confirmed some were student loans, she thought the student loans were showing up on her credit report because they were being paid late. I tried explaining several times they had never been late and how the credit report reflected all creditors – paid off ones, as well as currently opened accounts. But the mere mention of the student loans had her convinced there was some negative credit bureau reporting. I had a time convincing her not to pay off student loans because the rates were so low. But she insisted fearing her children were paying them late and marring her credit report.

When I finally convinced her not to include the student loans in the consolidation, my co-worker, overhearing our conversation, suggested she consider a home equity loan instead. "Why don't you just use a little equity from your house?" my co-worker asked. It sounded like a harmless cure-all and an ideal solution for an elderly couple in poor health with mounting medical bills. My customer certainly found that offer more enticing because it would give her enough cash back to pay off all her bills. She decided to go that route instead.

As I updated her information to determine if she qualified for a mortgage loan, I asked her the value of the house and how much she owed on it. She said it last appraised for $180,000 and she owed a little over $4,000 on it. The tax office confirmed the value and the credit bureau confirmed the amount owed. I said to her, "Ma'am, you've only got six payments left to pay off your house. Are you sure you want to get another mortgage on your house after paying for it for 30 years?" Even worse, her interest rate would have nearly doubled. Finally, I convinced her it wasn't such a good idea at her age.

She agreed to hold off until she had a chance to discuss it with her husband. Weeks later, he stopped by the office and explained why they needed the money. He said he had gone to the hospital for a fairly routine surgery after complaining about pain in his arm. But when he awakened in recovery, his entire left side was paralyzed. From the looks of him, you would have thought he had suffered a severe stroke or heart attack. That one misguided surgery left him disabled and out of work. It had also created an unmanageable mountain of hospital bills and prescription costs.

This articulate and intuitive victim of a negligent medical system, wasn't about to fall prey again to a just as broken financial system. He listened patiently as I explained the "deal" offered his wife. When he realized refinancing his nearly paid-off mortgage was not in their best interest, he said, "No thank you." And I sighed in relief.

Five Costly Dangers of Consolidating:

1) Ignoring interest rates: Always compare your old rates with the new rates being offered. Don't accept a new rate higher than what you have.

2) Borrowing more money than you need: Only get enough to pay off bills you have now, not debts you anticipate. Adding a few thousand dollars extra for maintenance

projects around the house will always appear logical and justifiable. But that will get you off track and more in debt.

3) Buying costly insurance on the loan: Insurances only ensure the lender will get paid should you default. Unemployment, disability and life insurance are cash cow investments for lenders, who rarely take time to explain the red tape and hoops you'll have to jump through to get the insurance company to take over your payments should you lose your job or become disabled. Plus, insurances can increase the loan balance by hundreds, if not thousands of dollars.

4) Using your car as collateral: NEVER secure a loan with your paid-off car or nearly paid-off car unless you can afford to lose it. When you borrow against your car, you're transferring ownership to the lender. If your loan payment goes 30 days past due, the lender can repossess your car, creating a double whammy for you – torn-up credit and no car. You can easily lose a $20,000 car for skipping payments on a $2,000 loan.

5) Co-signing for others: Co-signers are needed when a borrower doesn't have enough income to qualify, or has weak credit. By signing a contract as co-signer, you are agreeing to pay the loan if the primary borrower falls behind, regardless of the reason. Because you're linking their payment history to your credit report, if they pay poorly, it could ruin your credit. Proverbs 22:26 warns against co-signing debt.

What's worse is when non-qualifying customers can't find co-signers and don't have vehicles to secure loans, some lenders urge them to use someone else's car title to qualify. Using your title to secure someone's loan is just as dangerous as co-signing. People assume there's no harm in surrendering their titles because the non-obligor agreement they sign states they're under no obligation to pay the loan, which technically is true. But what's not clearly explained to them is if the borrower fails to pay, their vehicles may be repossessed. Especially if you're securing a loan with a vehicle far more valuable than the loan, not too many lenders would get bent out of shape if you stopped paying since the sale of your car would be more profitable. So if anyone asks to use your car title as collateral, run the other way!

One of the most important questions to ask when considering a loan is: "How much do I qualify for WITHOUT using my car or house as collateral?" Out of fear of being denied, consumers often secure loans with their property unnecessarily just because lenders suggest it. In actuality, based on their credit ratings and incomes alone, many qualify for unsecured loans. When consumers aren't aware of this, lenders capitalize on their ignorance, leveraging their vehicles to ensure timely payments.

Credit card balance transfers

We've all seen the enticing credit card offers that allow you to transfer balances of up to $20,000 to a new credit card account and receive a zero interest rate for the first six months. Then after the introductory period, the rate soars to 25 to 30 percent. The reason credit card companies can make such generous offers is only a handful of consumers actually pay their cards off during the introductory period, although many jump at those offers with that intention. Some companies include a pre-payment penalty to discourage customers from paying cards off during the introductory period.

Balance transfers should be approached with precaution. If there's a substantial savings in interest without penalty, it may be worthwhile. Too often customers fail to realize that although the offer says six months – no interest, interest is actually accruing on these accounts. It begins the day after the contract is signed; however, it is simply deferred for customers who consistently make on-time payments. With every missed or late payment, that interest is compounded. Nowhere in the contract does it say that no payments are due for six months. Consumers assume six-month-no-interest offers allow them six months to begin paying. But the first payment is due on the date outlined in the contract, and subsequent payments are due by that day every month thereafter. It's a debt trap baited to catch you.

Companies that finance furniture stores often offer similar arrangements. Their ads may indicate you can buy now and pay a year from now with no interest. But unless customers pay close attention to the loan's actual terms, due date, interest rate and premium – many are caught off guard when they learn their accounts are in default after a few months for nonpayment. Unfortunately, compounded interest and late fees constitute the bulk of the profits finance companies rake in. What could be more profitable than consumers who are totally ignorant of the terms in their contracts?

The zero-interest offers are among the most confusing in the industry. The ideal takers for these "deals" are people, anticipating large sums of money. They see nothing wrong with running out and financing furniture with plans of paying it off as soon as their income tax or bonus checks arrive. Since they're planning to pay it all off at once, so many innocently assume they can skip their regularly scheduled payments without penalty. If they had taken a moment to browse over the contract, they would see it mentions nothing about offering unconditional interest-free financing. The contract explains that as long as each premium is received by the due date, no interest will be charged for that month. But as soon as a payment is missed, you're slammed with interest and fees from the day after you signed the contract.

Chapter 3
Request Your Own Terms

There's no law requiring you to wait until creditors contact you with offers to help bring your accounts current. When you foresee a potential budget crisis that could affect your ability to pay, be proactive and call them. That signals them of your good intentions and your willingness to negotiate a solution that will save them money. Initiating the call places you in the driver's seat from which you can suggest terms – an interest rate and payment – that fit your budget.

When facing mortgage foreclosure, you've got to get aggressive. Since no one else is more adamant about saving your house than you, don't wait for the lender to call you. Contact your mortgage company and request a loan modification that will lower your payment and interest. But don't stop at getting the mortgage premium reduced. If you've got several delinquent accounts, why not request term adjustments from your other creditors too? Generally, when the mortgage is seriously delinquent, so is everything else. So don't assume, like many Americans, that if the mortgage payment is reduced, all the other bills will fall in place.

In many cases, it's not the mortgage but our undisciplined spending patterns that force us to live on the edge and without a budget. More than a few times, I've been the victim of my own emotional binge spending. Especially when I've had a terribly disappointing day, I felt entitled to run out and treat myself to something nice. But the short-term gain never outlasted the pain I incurred digging out from under a rash spending spree.

When facing a hardship, you should exercise your right to call each creditor and request a term adjustment that would make payments affordable. Having a mortgage company reduce the premium from $1,400 to $800 a month would significantly relieve pressure in many households. But that's only a drop in the bucket if your income has decreased 50 percent.

Even if you've already reduced your mortgage premium by 50 percent, it would be wise to request monthly payments lowered on a $600 car payment, $200 cell phone bill, $120 satellite bill and $600 in credit card bills. Those alone amount to $1,520 in bills, which don't include basic necessities like electricity, water, food, natural gas and fuel for the car. That's not to mention incidentals, unexpected repairs and health maintenance costs!

For most Americans our mortgage is our biggest debt, and being able to afford it helps ensure there will be a roof over our heads. But why stop there? If you're caught in a financial quandary, take the initiative and state your case before each creditor, requesting a lower interest rate and payment. If it's not your umpteenth request for help and they sense you're sincere about paying, you'll be surprised at the concessions they're willing to make. In 90 percent of cases, creditors will modify your loan. That is if your payment history shows you've had some integrity in paying them in the past. If you refused to pay when you were gainfully employed and money was rolling out of your pockets, creditors won't be as eager to help you. They quickly assess your payment history to determine if you're worth the risk.

They're more willing to bend for customers who use to pay consistently and on time. They will lengthen the term of your loan and only slightly reduce your interest rate in some cases. But lenders would much rather you continue paying a loan you can afford than for your debt to simply charge off after four months of nonpayment. Before approaching creditors, always pray and ask God to give you mercy and favor with them.

Charged off accounts can be as damaging to your credit report as filing bankruptcy, especially if you've got a slew of them. If left unsettled, charge offs usually disappear from your credit report after seven years. Bankruptcies can remain for as many as 10 years. But in today's market in which creditors are losing millions of dollars because of nonpayment, lenders and credit card companies are working feverishly to prevent accounts from charging off. Prior to 2008, most would have anxiously charged off a

$4,500 unsecured debt and recouped what they could from insurance companies. But now they're far more aggressive about taking borrowers to court.

Even for debts under $5,000, many companies are suing customers in small claims court and winning judgments against them. Others are resorting to wage garnishments. In states like North Carolina where only government agencies are authorized to garnish wages, credit card companies are filing liens against customers who own real estate, so that they can't sell or refinance their homes without paying the debt.

Always remember that the lender's job is to convince you that borrowing is the only sensible solution for coming out of debt. Borrowing and spending will NEVER catapult you out of debt! No matter how good it looks on paper or sounds on television ads, it does not work and never will.

According to Proverbs 22:7, "The borrower is servant to the lender." Based on the law of reciprocity, we will reap what we sow. That means it's impossible to sow debt and reap prosperity.

Deferments are not your Friends

Every time you bring an account current by deferring a payment, or pushing it to the end of the loan, you're simply stockpiling compounded interest and fees. You are adding to each deferred payment an extra day of interest for every day left on your loan. In other words, daily interest is accruing on your total loan balance, as well as on each skipped payment and its fees. For example, if you are a month late making a $200 loan payment and agree to have it deferred, you'll be charged interest and late fees for being 30 days late, interest on the total loan balance, plus interest for every day that deferred $200 payment sits at the end of your loan. Can you imagine what a train wreck you're creating at the end of your loan by deferring five or more payments?

One long-term customer I called to offer a loan put it this way: "Ms. Patterson, since I took out that loan, I've put two children through college, paid off a car and truck, and I'm still trying to pay your company back $3,000." We both burst into laughter. Although humorous, his analogy was typical. Between compounded deferred interest, fees and add-on loans, it looked like he would never be able to pay the thing off. When I offered more money, he usually gave in saying, "What the heck, I could use a few extra dollars." In a commission environment, this type customer was an easy sell. So my goal was keeping him at his loan limit.

If you occasionally pay more than the amount due on a personal loan, the extra money accumulates toward the next payment. So if your budget gets tight, rather than request a deferment, simply ask the account representative how much is required to "move" or "advance" your account. Sometimes, only a few dollars are needed to bring accounts current.

It's just as important to ask the right question when trying to determine what you owe on an account. Ask for a payoff balance, instead of inquiring about the number of payments left. You can't always determine the amount owed by the number of payments remaining. Some of the most abusive customers I've had were slow payers who calculated their debt based on the number of payments left. When they learned they had only a few payments but still owed thousands of dollars, many went ballistic. One auto customer with two payments left had a payoff balance of over $8,000. But whose fault was it that he, like many customers, had asked the wrong question?

When you ask how many payments are left, you're inquiring about the payments remaining to fulfill the term of your loan contract. Unless you've made every payment on time, this may have no correlation to the amount you owe. If your loan is financed for 60 months, when the 58th month rolls around, you've technically got two monthly payments left to pay off your loan, regardless of how much you owe.

This confuses so many consumers, who figure if they are paying $200 a month and have only two payments left, their payoff is automatically around $400. That's because they have no clue as to the damaging potholes refinances and "skipped" or deferred payments are stabbing into their loan balances. Look at it this way, if deferred payments weren't such a golden treasure trove for lenders, all the busywork associated with tracking payments that roll to the end of loans wouldn't be worth their while. But the real question is what's in it for you? Besides prolonged compounded debt, heartache and short-term convenience, absolutely nothing.

The Hammer Method

I believe the most effective and rewarding way to pay off debts is to knock them down one by one, using what I call the hammer method. Picture your financial portfolio as a wooden foundation covered with protruding nails. In order to keep the foundation standing, each nail must be securely fastened to the wood. Starting with the smallest nail, you should hammer each one until its head is fitting tightly against the wood, leaving no room for it to snag anything or wiggle loose. The nails in this method are your bills.

Here's how it works: List each of your bill balances from lowest to highest. Then, pay only your absolute essentials: mortgage or rent, childcare, car note, transportation to work, utilities and the minimum balances on credit cards and loans. If your income permits, set aside a minimal amount ($50 to $100 per pay period or per month) as a miscellaneous fund. Apply every dime left after paying your bills to your smallest account balance. Once that account is paid off, go to the next account and do the same thing. Every time you pay an account off, you'll have more money to apply to the next bill on your list. Just make sure you don't misapply the extra money to your miscellaneous fund. This isn't the time to reward yourself.

Since this method allocates no money for restaurants or entertainment, you'll need to skip or minimize eating out and become creative in preparing foods in your house. Or feel free to designate half of your miscellaneous fund to food. But once this fund is spent, you must be determined not to withdraw additional money from the bank. You'll be surprised at how quickly you are able to pay off balances under $5,000. Not only will this method require that you make a substantial sacrifice, but more importantly, it will help you develop the discipline needed to stay out of debt.

Buying or Refinancing a Home

A market brimming with foreclosed properties offers prime opportunities for buying a house. Because banks and finance companies are more anxious to get rid of repossessed homes, homebuyers, who take time to shop around for what they want, will find that they have a lot more bargaining power. By continuing to use the hammer method once bills are paid off, you can easily set aside a sizeable down payment on a house at below-market costs. If you can save 20 percent of the mortgage balance as a down payment, that will reduce your monthly premium by 5 percent because you won't have to pay Premium Mortgage Insurance (PMI).

Mortgage finance companies add PMI to the payments for the first six years to ensure that they get their money if your loan goes into foreclosure. If your down payment is less than 20 percent, keep track of the amount you pay each year, because once you've paid 20 percent, or after five years have passed, you can request that PMI is dropped. Not knowing this can cause you to pay for an extra year of unnecessary insurance.

However, the biggest money saver if you are financing a new house will come from immediately tipping the interest scale in your favor. This little trick is one of the industry's best-kept secrets. Because it generates hundreds of billions of dollars each year, it is one that finance companies are careful not to leak. All you have to do is make your first payment the day after you close your loan. That payment would hit your new loan account before one day of interest accrues on it, which means every penny of that payment would go to principal. But make sure you make this payment discreetly.

Announcing your plan in advance to your lender or real estate agent could possibly lead to roadblocks. Because of the losses they would incur, lenders often stall for time to rewrite your loan, so that they can incorporate that first payment into your down payment. Making the first payment 45 days early on a 30-year mortgage could instantly knock years off your loan. Have you ever noticed that whenever you've borrowed money, the finance company gives you about 45 days to begin making your first payment?

If you're borrowing in December, the lender will tell you they're giving you extra time, so you'll have plenty of money for Christmas. If you're borrowing in July, they tell you the extra time is to help you enjoy your vacation or Fourth of July holiday. Whenever you borrow, they always come up with a line to explain why there's a 45-day wait before your first payment's due. No one will ever admit to you that it's designed to allow them to accrue 45 days of interest on your loan.

The truth is the only reason you're given 45 days to make your first payment is because legally, that's the only way they can add a whopping 45 days of accrued interest to the top of your loan. That may not seem like very much on a $500 recliner you're financing. But it tallies up pretty quickly when added to the top of a $150,000 to $200,000 mortgage with a 5 percent interest rate. We're talking some serious ducats now. That's why if you wait and pay on their schedule, not one red penny of your first payment goes to principal. Every dime goes to interest.

Obviously, the more you pay the day after closing, the more you save. To make sure this payment is credited for the proper date, it's best to make it at the start of the business day in person or by phone and to get the name and title of the person posting it. If told your payment can't be posted because the loan is still being processed and isn't setup in the system, insist that it's credited for that day, and carefully review your receipt. If posted by phone, ask if a confirmation number can be manually generated. When you send a payment by mail before your account is added to the system, lenders sometimes pretend not to understand why the money has been sent despite the fact they can link it to the mountain of paperwork you completed. No matter how explicitly you've documented your request in a note, they will stall posting it to try to minimize their losses on the front end.

To save even more money on a new mortgage, continue paying the loan ahead of schedule. Make subsequent payments every 30 days from the first payment. For example, if your loan closed on March 1, and your first payment is due April 15, you would make your first payment on March 2 and subsequent payments on April 2, May 2, June 2 and so on. Auto drafts are the easiest way to keep payments on track and avoid extra interest. But make sure your mortgage company withdraws on the date you specify, rather than on the due date. If you get paid twice a month, it may be convenient to draft half a payment each payday. Some banks don't permit biweekly or twice-a-month payments. Others may allow it if you have a checking or savings account with them, but charge a handling fee.

Chapter 4
Don't Love Money

One of the worse mistakes we make is allowing money to define our worth in society, and we unconsciously allow it to regulate our joy. When my ex-husband and I decided to separate, I was consumed with fear over how I would stay afloat. Although I've always been a conservative spender, I didn't know how I would provide for my young son and daughter. My ex had paid the mortgage and part of the utilities, and my salary paid for our children's tuition at a Christian school, the rest of the utilities, my car payment and the joint credit card bill he continued to run up.

He had announced he was keeping the house and the children and that I was free to leave at any time with my clothes and half of the furniture. Although we had built that house and lived there for 10 years, I was willing to let him keep it, but I wasn't about to give up my children. Angry, depressed and overwhelmed, I started apartment hunting. With everything I was going through, I needed a safe haven, so I began my search in southeast Charlotte, one of the safest areas of the city. I thought surely the rent would be much cheaper than our mortgage. Boy! Was I out of touch! I had no idea the cost of housing had risen so drastically in just 10 years. Even the barest one-bedroom apartments were priced beyond my reach. Flabbergasted and depressed about not being able to afford anything, I got in my car and went back home.

I made a counseling appointment with my pastor whom I'd confided in over the years. To my surprise, he was quite supportive when I told him of my plans to file for divorce. He looked a bit puzzled though when I mentioned to him that I had been apartment hunting.

"Why are you leaving your house?" he asked. "You should stay there, and let him find another place to live. You've got the children," he said as if trying to convince me that what he said made sense. Ding, ding, ding...a wake-up bell finally sounded in my head, and a little light shone. For the first time, some hope had filtered through my befuddled mind racked with divorce planning. Those were the most comforting words I had heard in a long time. They forced me to suddenly realize I had just as much right to keep the house as he did – actually a little more since I would remain the primary guardian of our two children. That was just the boost I needed to set an appointment with an attorney to get the ball rolling.

I told the attorney upfront that I wanted to keep the house, and that my ex could have everything in it. But the attorney advised against that settlement, arguing it wouldn't be an equitable distribution. He told me I'd wind up on the short end of the stick if I awarded my spouse all the furnishings in the house, the newer vehicle and his entire pension.   He urged me to instead go after half of the furnishings and half of his pension. He said if I didn't want the furnishings to at least go after half the pension.

"His pension is far more valuable than your little house," he explained.

That comment set off another warning bell in my head. It made me realize the lawyer wasn't as concerned about my wellbeing as he was about his own pocket. He had a chance to get paid a whole lot more if I agreed to go after the pension instead of the house. I was holding onto a 10-year-old unfinished prefab split level with a $55,000 mortgage balance. He was offering me twice as much in pension proceeds. On the surface, it sounded like a lucrative deal. Many would have called it a no brainer. But while the attorney stressed his ability to liquidate my ex's retirement assets, he evaded questions about when I would be eligible to receive payment from them. The truth is that company pensions can't be fully liquidated until an employee officially retires, which in this case would have been 15 years later. Generally, the only other time pensions pay is when employees die – a death benefit is paid to the dependent children or spouse.

I figured by the time my ex retired, I should be pretty well situated, and if he died before then, his pension would just go to my children. Rather than settle for pie in the sky, I just wanted to hold onto my house. Regardless of how stupid the attorney tried to make me feel, I wasn't giving up my house. Had I been enticed by greed with the attorney's offer, I could have made a decision that would have set my children and me back for years – living hand-to-mouth. The lawyer's plan gave me only two options – to sell the house and give my ex half the proceeds, which would have forced me to find a place for us to live, adding to the instability and confusion my children were already facing. The other option was for me to borrow half the appraised value of the house to buy my ex out. Both options would have prolonged my case, requiring me to pay the lawyer a much higher percentage in legal fees. At that time on my small salary, the last thing I needed was a loan payment on top of my mortgage and other bills.

Not only did I stick with my original plan, but once I got through the equitable distribution hearing, I got rid of the lawyer. I knew I didn't need him after waiting a few hours in court for him to make a 10-minute appearance. For that appearance he charged me hundreds of dollars plus a retainer. I realized that with the help of the Lord, I could come out a lot cheaper handling the rest of my case myself. I was determined to reduce my out-of-pocket costs. I went to the public library and looked up samples of local divorce court documents. After reviewing the wording and format for several, I selected one, copied it and used it to format my own. Representing myself actually saved me thousands of dollars. Surprisingly, my documents looked just as professional and authentic as any attorney's.

With no attorney present the judge reviewed them, signed them and declared the divorce official.

God had freed me from a stressful relationship and maneuvered me around a huge legal debt trap.

Chapter 5
Talk like You're Winning

The desires, thoughts and imaginations that dominate our spirits will sooner or later become reality in our lives. Everything exists in the spirit world first. When we're distressed and overly burdened emotionally, it can sometimes appear to be the other way around. It may seem like everyday circumstances control our spirits, causing us to feel fear, anger or joy. Actually, the words we speak create a spiritual force, which determines whether we win or lose. That's because death and life are in the power of the tongue.

When I was going through a bad marriage, plants wouldn't grow in my house. They sat in a prime spot right beneath a window with plenty of sunlight beaming down on them. Yet every plant I touched or just left to fend for itself withered and died within months. It was as if the plants reflected my negative words and spiritual temperament. I felt rejected, abandoned and hurt, and my conversation reflected that. No matter what I did to those plants, I got no positive response... no glimmer of hope or spark of life from them. When guests complimented my plants, I'd respond with something like: "I just bought that.

Within a few months, it'll be dead. My plants never live longer than a few months."

I continued getting exactly what I said – plants that died after a few months. Now why I continued replacing them remains a mystery even to me. But several months after my ex moved out, my whole attitude changed. I began listening to more teaching tapes on finances, health, raising children... you name it. Also, I began speaking more positively (Proverbs 18:21). Finally, I became confident in the fact that God could take care of my children and me all by Himself. That's when things really began to turn around. I felt a freedom that I hadn't felt in 10 years. I began walking around my little house uninhibited with out-stretched arms singing and praising God for His goodness.

One by one God began working things out for me. He began causing everything I touched to flourish – from my equitable distribution settlement right down to my house plants sitting under the dining room window. They were the same types of plants sitting in the same spots. The lighting hadn't changed, and I wasn't watering them any more frequently. More often than not, I'd forget to water them at all. Yet they flourished. Even the Dieffenbachia was about to grow through my ceiling. What changed was the spiritual atmosphere of my household. When I began praising God without knowing exactly what the future held, God restored my joy. Although at times I was challenged with fear, I sensed His love for me and knew everything would be alright. Psalm 22:3 explains that God inhabits the praises of His people.

It's not unusual to hear people overwhelmed by debt respond as if they have no hope for change. As believers we can't afford to murmur and complain about the economy as if our trust is in this broken economic system. I used to complain sometimes just because I could. But when it finally registered in my spirit that I had the power to create life or destroy life with my tongue, I became a lot more conscious about the words I spoke over myself and my children.

Years ago, as I studied for the National Mortgage Licensing Service exam, I constantly confessed that I would pass it the first time around. But as I sat in the testing center about 10 minutes into the exam, I was so overwhelmed by the level of difficulty that I just wanted to scream, cuss and walk out. I had been studying for months and was totally frustrated because the three-day course the company had provided covered only a fraction of the topics included on the exam.

When I bowed my head and closed my eyes to silently pray, I heard these words in my spirit: "Don't forget who you are." Immediately, I apologized to the Lord for becoming so angry and for a moment, forgetting everything I had confessed. I reminded Him that I belonged to Him and that I could do all things through Christ who strengthened me. I told Him that I have the mind of Christ, and I thanked Him for going before me on that test and making every crooked place straight. Lastly, I thanked Him for passing that exam for me, although I had only answered the first 10 of the 50 questions. Since it was a timed exam, I couldn't spend too much time praying, so I raised my head and resumed testing. By the grace of God, I passed by two points.

Out of the company's 188 loan originators in the Carolinas, I was one of the few who passed the exam the first time around. Folks with five times my tenure have taken it over a dozen times without success. But had I spoken one word out of my frustration, I would have cancelled all the faith-filled confessions I had made while preparing for the exam. Although I hadn't anticipated the exam being so difficult, I should not have lost my focus on God's ability to help me pass it. But once I regained my spiritual focus and realigned my words with His words instead of my emotions, He was able to pull me through. The same spiritual principle applies to our finances. Sadly, by the time the much easier state exam rolled around, I thought I knew enough to pass it without making confessions. As a result, I wound up having to take it a second time.

That's why it's so important for us to remind ourselves daily to say what God says about our situations. That not only builds our faith, it helps us to trust God's integrity.

Sometimes, I've forgotten to act on confessions I've made. But without faith it is impossible to please God (Hebrews 11:6). Sometimes, our emotions have dominated our minds, especially when we're saying the same thing over and over but seeing no results. That's when we've got to keep speaking our faith, because faith comes by hearing God's word, whether it's from our own lips or from someone else's.

For this reason, we should never make faithless confessions such as: "I'm broke. I can't afford that. I don't have enough money. My money's tight. I'll never get this bill paid off. Every time I catch up, something goes wrong. That cost me an arm and a leg." These comments totally contradict every promise God has made to prosper us. Although God's plan was to prosper the children of Israel, we see in Exodus that they wandered 40 years in the wilderness because they constantly accused God of bringing them out of Egypt to kill them. God simply allowed them to have what they continuously said.

The government is not the answer

During tough economic times, many Americans put their faith in the president or a political party to come up with an easy solution for their personal financial crises. Even some Christians are banking on legislation passing that would relieve them of their responsibility to pay their creditors. The problem is this legislation would do nothing to curb reckless out-of-control spending. That's how

America became indebted to the tune of trillions of dollars in the first place. That's not faith. That's a something-for-nothing mentality. No single presidential administration put us in this position, and no one administration can pull us out. Under the burden of debt, the world's financial system is crumbling right before our eyes.

Without a sovereign act of God and a divinely inspired plan to balance our nation's budget, our government will never see a balanced budget. But the good news is, unless you choose to, nobody has to go down with a sinking ship. Even if all the life rafts are occupied, we all have the right to jump overboard. But once off the ship, those who are better prepared will have the option of swimming for their lives, while the only hope of surviving for many others will be to grab hold of a secure object and wait to be rescued. Throughout time, even in the severest of circumstances, God sustained and prospered those willing to swim against the tide, trusting Him as their refuge.

As Moses marched the children of Israel toward the Red Sea, those in his own camp started questioning his sanity because all circumstances were against them. The fierce waves of that vast body of water probably created images of drowning. As they stood between two death traps – Pharaoh's army behind them and the Red Sea in front of them – the Israelites could not afford to become paralyzed by fear. Although they saw no possibility of surviving either treacherous condition, they coaxed themselves into moving forward in spite of what they saw. Once they moved forward, God stepped in and delivered every one of them. He wants to do the same for us.

Chapter 6
Downsize is Not a Dirty Word

Whether creditors modify your debts to fit within your budget or not, the next logical step is to downsize. Ask yourself, "What do I need to eliminate?" If you're paying a cell phone bill for an adolescent or younger child, that bill should be at the top of your hit list. In most cases, that's purely a luxury that serves no practical purpose. Unless you work for a cable network or satellite company, the next logical bill to eliminate may be cable TV or your subscription to a satellite dish service. Sadly, most men would rather skip naked down Wall Street during rush hour than to be stuck at home with their wives for a weekend with no cable. But eliminating this bill could quickly generate a lot of cash, especially toward a past-due mortgage. Besides, without the TV constantly blaring in your ears, you might have time for uninterrupted discussions with the children or spouse.

Other luxuries you might consider eliminating are gym or social club memberships and lawn services. By investing in an inexpensive lawn mower, you can save tons of money on lawn services, plus get plenty of healthy cardiovascular exercise cutting your own grass. The chart below guestimates how much you could save per month by getting rid of nonessentials. It's based on a random sampling of friends and associates in the Charlotte metropolitan area.

Cable TV/Satellite Service	$125
Extra Cell phone	$90
Publication subscriptions	$35
Gym Membership	$75
Lawn Service	$200
Lunchtime Dining Out	$140
Nail services	$60
Car washes	$60
Spa/Salon Services	$150
Soft drinks	$30
Extra vehicles	Blue Book Value

No sacred stashes

Again, the most cost-effective way to pay down debt is to first tap into your own reserves. We all have something that we can turn into quick cash, whether it's an account, collectable treasures or unused skills and services that lay dormant. The question is: How willing are we to part with our time and/or possessions to put a dent in our debt? Don't feel compelled to answer that question just yet. If you guardedly cherish your time, considering it just as valuable as your disposable cash, trust me, you're not alone. So for now, let's take a look at your other assets, like the big glaring interest-bearing accounts that we peek at but wouldn't dare touch – IRAs, CDs, stocks and bonds, company retirement plans and college savings accounts.

Sadly, many treat these as sacred stashes that are as make-believe as Monopoly money. As a result, these accounts sit idly by accumulating thousands of dollars in interest toward retirement or an infant's college tuition, while their owners face mortgage foreclosure and a barrage of creditors trying to force them into bankruptcy. There's no better time to tap into company pensions and retirement funds we've squirreled away than when faced with a real emergency. Although some employers don't provide emergency cash advances, many allow employees to borrow against their retirement accounts and pay themselves back with minimal interest.

Because of the whopping tax penalties for withdrawing IRAs prematurely, you should only consider cashing them when faced with a real emergency, such as a mortgage foreclosure or costly life-threatening medical needs. Before withdrawing one dime from an IRA, make sure you clearly understand the penalty you'll pay up front and at tax time. If you had to withdraw $60,000 from an IRA to save your house, you can avoid surprises by finding out how much the IRS will penalize you at tax time.

All of our lives, most baby boomers were advised to never touch the sacred funds set aside for retirement. That advice, which was so applicable during economic boom times, does not apply in today's economy. It ranks right up there with the adage, "pay yourself first." Both have confused a lot of people. Years ago, "pay yourself first" was sound advice, but it was advice basically intended for people whose bills weren't drastically behind. The idea was for them to set aside a savings account to be used for emergency or "rainy day" expenses, or even for leisure. It didn't make a lick of sense then, and still doesn't, for those whose bills were already months behind.

If your bills are past due and you're regularly stashing aside large sums in savings accounts, you are actually creating your own "rainy days." You're accumulating unnecessary interest on debts you owe and prolonging paying off accounts that may have been paid off or paid down with money you've stashed away. As a result, you wind up paying the finance company $33,000 back on the

$10,000 you borrowed. That's anything but good stewardship and definitely money that in most cases could be put to better use. I'm not saying don't save at all.

Setting aside a small sum that you won't miss is not a bad idea. But going in debt to do it is. Also, it's dishonest to skip paying creditors while hoarding money in savings for expenses we anticipate. Instead, any extra money should be used to bring accounts current. After all, when we apply for credit, we actually sign a legal contract stating that we will honor our commitment by making a payment every 30 days on or before the due date. We also acknowledge the company's right to take legal action should we fail to fulfill our end of the bargain.

As I listened to a financial advisor on the radio, a widow in her mid to late 50's called seeking advice. Although she worked three jobs, she was barely making ends meet and under a lot of stress. Because she was struggling to pay her $160,000 first mortgage and a $60,000 second mortgage, she wanted to know if she should withdraw part of the $300,000 stashed in her 401K to pay off one of the mortgages. I was totally floored by the advisor's response. He told her not to touch the $300,000 she had saved, but to instead search for a better job. He obviously felt her health wasn't nearly as valuable as her savings account.

This dear lady was working her body in the ground and paying interest on $220,000 in mortgages while drawing interest on $300,000 in savings. Even if she just paid off the first mortgage, she would have relieved the pressure. Instead the advisor regarded the $300,000 savings as if it were her only source of survival, and once it was depleted, she'd be totally up the creek. In his mind, God couldn't possibly meet her future needs without her 401K. But if the earth is the Lord's and everything in it, you'd better believe God's not broke. When we trust Him and try to handle money properly, He's obligated to take care of His own. Tapping into investment accounts in an emergency could possibly improve our health and extend our lives.

No sacred treasures

Let's say you've searched your accounts, along with all the missing money websites and realize you have no hidden-away, lost or forgotten money. The next practical step is to ask yourself, "What's in my house that I can sell?" Begin this exercise by taking inventory of the items that you own in your house. Jot down everything you're honestly willing to part with. Beside each item, write down what you feel is the depreciated value – the amount you believe someone would be willing to pay for it. Then, beside that write your realistic wish list amount – the amount you wish you could receive from the sale of that item. Then average the two prices to come up with your fair list price.

There are many popular social websites such as Craigslist and EBay that you could list your items on. However, if you live alone, you might want to set up a public meeting place to avoid inviting strangers into your home. Or you may want to host a yard sale, which would allow you to wheel and deal, negotiate one-on-one and reduce prices to ensure a sale. If you enjoy working solo, you could do it alone. Otherwise, you may find motivation in having others participate.

Regardless of how little or how much you make from the sale, stay focused. Aside from your tithes, all proceeds should go toward paying off existing bills, not toward creating new ones. Even if you make a bundle, you defeat the purpose if you begin eyeing your excess as vacation money or a Christmas fund.

If needed, prized coin collections and precious jewelry from family heirlooms could be liquidated too. Often, we safely tuck away stuff that we'd dare not wear anywhere waiting for it to appreciate and hoping not to lose it. Aside from gathering dust and age, old coins aren't of any value until they're exchanged for cash. In a financial pinch, they could become much more valuable if sold to cover a mortgage payment.

Hidden costs add up

In a typical household, there are almost always hidden costs that inconspicuously gnaw away at a budget. Sometimes, we get so accustomed to paying them, we don't think twice about whether or not we actually need the services. Among the biggest money leeches in this category are insurances and warranties. Many find peace of mind in being overly insured. If you're driving a 10-year-old car but have enough money in the bank to replace it, there's no need to carry full auto insurance coverage on it. Full coverage may be practical on a 10-year-old luxury car or classic, or on mid-sized models that depreciate slowly, such as Hondas and Volkswagens.

The North Carolina Department of Motor Vehicles requires only liability insurance on vehicles that are paid off. Consumers are not required to resume full coverage unless they use their paid-off vehicles as security for a loan. In that case, if you fail to restore collision coverage, the lender will add forced-place insurance, which is usually more costly. Because drivers sometimes forget to adjust insurance coverage when their needs decline, they wind up paying far more to carry full coverage than they would recoup if their cars were totaled.

Auto Warranties

A good way to lower your car payment and shorten your loan payoff is to eliminate costly extended warranties. Most major parts are covered by the manufacturer's warranty for the first three years. Especially in today's market, buyers should be wary of slick auto sales people who add costly warranties into the monthly premiums, but cancel them once they've collected their commissions.

That happened to me several years ago when I bought an SUV. After I began experiencing electrical problems, I learned my warranty had been cancelled without my authorization. The dealer admitted the salesman had cancelled it, but said he had left the company, and there was nothing they could do about it. I wound up covering the repairs out of pocket. Shortly after that, my income was reduced, making it difficult for me to juggle the car payment with my mortgage and other bills. Realizing I could no longer afford the monthly car payment, I prayed about it. In my spirit I knew I had to downsize. I tried to find a buyer at work, but nobody wanted it. So I took a day off and went from one dealership to another offering to trade down for a small, less expensive car. But they all told me the same thing, which was they couldn't accept a vehicle with an $18,000 balance as a trade-in.

Finally, when I was about to walk out of the fifth or sixth dealership, I explained to an old salesman that I had been to nearly every major dealership on Charlotte's east side trying to get rid of my car. He said, "Honey, no dealership's going to buy that car. You owe too much on it. Why don't you take it down there to CarMax? They'll buy it from you and give you what you owe on it."

I was so happy about that news I could have kissed him. After thanking him, I grabbed my daughter and rushed down the street to CarMax. Within minutes, their mechanic had my car on the rack evaluating it. Thirty minutes later, a service manager walked over to me, told me the most they could offer me was $18,000 and asked if I accepted the offer. I was ecstatic. Then he wanted to know if I could sign the paperwork that day to get my check. At first, I said "yes," until it dawned on me I didn't have transportation to get home or to work the next day. So I asked him to give me a week to find another car. When I got home, I prayed and asked the Lord to lead me to a reasonable durable used car in excellent condition for $6,000 or less.

A few days later, I bought a used Toyota Corolla that I had seen in the paper and immediately took it to Toyota for a diagnostic exam. After checking it out, the mechanic told me, "The bad news is you've got a cracked distributor cap. The good news is it's covered by your warranty."

Sounding a little disappointed, I explained to him that I was not the car's original owner since I had just bought it and hadn't received any extended warranty documents. He told me that didn't matter because all engine work was covered by the manufacturer's warranty and that replacing it wouldn't cost me one dime. All I could say was, "Thank you, Jesus!" I was ready to shout about then. I believe God worked that situation out because I obeyed Him by downsizing. I didn't even have to pay the diagnostic charge.

Generally, the manufacturer's warranty covers appliances, electronics and household equipment from one to two years, and defects are usually detected within the first few years. Seldom is there a need to buy extended warranties on household appliances.

Conserve on Utilities

Another money leech is wasted electricity. We can shut the door to this debt trap by conscientiously unplugging computers, modems, routers, televisions, DVD players, electronic games, radios, unused clocks, microwaves, coffee makers, dental hygiene equipment and other small appliances and household electronics when not in use. Doing so can put a sizeable dent in an electric bill. Because of all the computerized gadgets built into our electronics, most continue to burn electricity even when they're turned off. When plugged into a socket, small items like cell phone chargers continue to burn electricity even when no phone's plugged in.

If you want to see a fragile household wallowing around a debt trap, just observe people who use no restraint in operating utilities. I bet you've visited folks like that, and some are even relatives. They complain about escalating heating costs. But take one step in the door of their homey little infernos, and heat darn near singes your eyebrows. It's like stepping into a furnace. Despite the fact it's brutally cold outside in mid-February, everyone inside sits around in T-shirts and shorts, barefoot and congested. When the temperature drops to 30 degrees, their thermostats are set on 80, even while they're asleep. And when it rises to 95, the thermostat's set to 65. They may be struggling to keep a roof over their heads, but contend the one place they're entitled to be comfortable is in their own castles.

Rather than wait for a serious economic downswing to force you to conserve energy, get in the habit now of setting your thermostat below your comfort threshold. Practicing this simple survival technique will force your body to more easily adapt to sudden severe temperature changes. If you're comfortable heating with your thermostat at 75 during the day and 72 for bed at night, practice setting it five degrees lower -- 70 during the day and 67 degrees at night. Until your body adjusts, you may want to dress in layers. I find the cool, crisp air refreshing, and it helps me sleep more comfortably.

If a room has sufficient sunlight or is unoccupied, I unconsciously turn off the lights. My challenge is remembering not to do that when visiting others. It drives relatives up a wall when I unconsciously flip their light switches off. They're so accustomed to glaring lights and noisy TV backgrounds throughout the night that when one suddenly goes off, it unnerves them.

Nonetheless, according to monthly reports from the electric company, my bill is 40 to 50 percent less than those of nearby residents with houses about the same size, which proves this cost-cutting measure is paying off. I also reduce costs by using my dishwasher only on holidays or after large dinner gatherings. Aside from garments I wash by hand, I limit washing clothes to once a week and towels and linens to once every two or three weeks. Practically all my washing is done on a permanent press or delicate cycle with cold water, using a potent laundry detergent.

Eating economically

Cutting back may not require eliminating eating out altogether. But it does require relying on God's wisdom. When we rely on Him, He shows us how to save money, where to find bargains and even how to eat on a budget. For those who live alone, it's not always convenient to buy foods and prepare them yourself. I enjoy eating out occasionally, but I try not to spend extravagantly on meals. My goal is to eat healthier and to consume more life-sustaining foods, rather than those loaded with artificial sweeteners and additives. I used to grab a fast-food meal and dash home to eat lunch until I realized my full-course meal at a buffet was cheaper than a combination meal (sandwich, fries and drink) at a fast-food restaurant.

I was shocked when my takeout lunch at a buffet came to less than $5. I had a healthy helping of string beans, perch, sweet potatoes and zucchini, which was more than enough. The cashier had advised me I'd come out a lot cheaper paying $10.99 for the buffet takeout special, which included a drink. I thanked her and explained I preferred weighing my food. Had I taken her suggestion, I would have paid $7 more for the same meal.

I couldn't help but wonder why I hadn't realized how reasonable it was to eat a healthy lunch out before. One deterrent might have been that cashiers generally recommend the higher buffet package over weighing your food, and normally, I took their word. But that day, I learned the key to breaking the buffet, rather than letting it break me. It all centers around eating normal portions – only putting on your plate what you would ordinarily eat at home or at a full-service restaurant. Packing food on a plate in layers deep enough to divvy out to the Carolina Panthers' line defeats the purpose. In that case, weighing it for takeout would cost a lot more than eating in the restaurant.

For me another cost saver when purchasing restaurant food to go is deciding what I want to eat before I arrive, especially at a buffet. That way I'm not wandering from station to station like a hungry ox in a stall, waiting to pounce on whatever comes out of the kitchen. Deciding beforehand and sticking to it prevents me from being gluttonous. It's when I've gone in starving and undecided about what I wanted that I've overeaten. Next thing you know you're saying: "Wow, the liver and onions smell so good. The meatloaf looks delicious. That fried chicken looks so tender and so does the steak and fish. I think I'll try them all."

Creatures of habit

Store brand products and online coupons offer great savings on groceries. Since I had used one brand of laundry detergent, dish detergent and toilet paper since childhood, I wasn't terribly open to trying other brands because I assumed they were inferior. That was until I learned how much cheaper store brands could be. I also learned that neither all store brands, nor name brands were created equally.

When I moved to Charlotte from the Midwest, my roommate insisted her 1,000-sheet bathroom tissue lasted twice as long as my favorite name brand. She challenged me to a few month-long tests to see which lasted longer. To my surprise, hers lasted nearly twice as long as mine. So I switched to her brand, and to this day, I buy it whenever it's on sale or its comparable store brand. Many major manufacturers distribute their products under a generic label at cheaper prices, and aside from packaging, there's no difference in the product. I used a different brand of paper towels. But when money was tight, I set out cloth towels instead.

I found tons of bargains at grocery stores offering only the bare basics. These no-frills stores often operate out of warehouses and have low advertising and operating costs. Many don't provide free bags or shopping carts, so I was surprised by the number of high-quality products they offered, like organic canned vegetables and large Grade A eggs from grain-fed hens that had not been injected with growth hormones. If you're not married to methods and willing to venture a little out of your box, you'll see that bargains will sometimes find you.

Whenever we're overwhelmed with debt and seek God's direction, He almost always instructs us to stop borrowing, downsize and sow financial seeds to bless others. Because of the law of reciprocity, the point discussed in the next chapter is one of the most important keys to coming out of debt.

Chapter 7
Get Ready to Sow & Reap

When I joined my church in 1985, services were held at a conference center owned by a Holiday Inn in north Charlotte. We kicked off a building project to raise over a million dollars for a new sanctuary. I was amazed to see funds raised solely through tithes and offerings – no bake sales, no chicken dinners, no raffles or rallies, no car washes or any of the methods used by churches I had previously attended. Since the construction was pay-as-you-go, it took us a few years, but once completed, we marveled at the new debt-free multi-purpose facility complete with an eleven-hundred-seat sanctuary, full-scale gym and bowling alley.

Members shared one testimony after another about how God multiplied their finances through extra hours at work, part-time jobs, promotions and unexpected funds, so that they could consistently give extra money above their tithes to the building project. By the time the project was completed, our congregation had tripled in size and outgrown the new building. After expanding to three

Sunday morning services, we launched a new building project for a much larger facility.

After hearing all the testimonies from the first project, I couldn't wait to give toward the second building fund. As I gave extra money above my tithes, God multiplied my finances again and again. Although I had been a journalist since college, at the time, I was in between jobs working crazy hours as a long distance phone company operator. While I was grateful I had a job, I hated it, and God knew it. As I continued to give my tithes and offerings into the ministry, He blessed me with a job as a business writer for a local newspaper. Not only did it pay more, the hours were 8 a.m. to 5 p.m. Monday through Friday, plus I really liked the work, my boss and my environment.

Combine Confession with Sowing and Reaping

Years had passed since PTL, the Charlotte area evangelical empire, had fallen. The ministry headquarters was situated on over a thousand acres of land with its own television studios, theme park, water park, mall, hotels and subdivisions. In its heyday, it was an ideal spot for Christian families seeking to get away for a wholesome family-oriented retreat or vacation where children could roam the grounds and play safely. Various ministries and partnerships tried unsuccessfully to purchase the property headed into bankruptcy with hopes of revitalizing portions of the dream brought to life by Jim Bakker. But all attempts failed. Finally, Morris Cerullo Ministries launched a national television campaign to raise money to buy PTL's broadcasting operations.

I was thrilled about the possibility of the property once again thriving in Christian hands and desperately wanted to support the buyback. But after the birth of my daughter, I had been at home with her for months and dependent on my husband's income. I knew he didn't want a dime of his money going toward the project, so I made a small pledge of $100. Then I had to figure out how I would earn money to pay it. Around that time, I heard a message on the power of confession that urged job seekers to, "stop looking for a job" and "go get a job." I told my family I was going to get a job. The first and only place I went, I got hired on the spot. I had gotten ready that Monday morning, dressed my toddler and drove about 10 minutes from my house to apply for a job at a company that produced school yearbooks.

My husband was at work, and I didn't have extra money to pay for a babysitter, so I took my daughter with me. The receptionist confirmed the company was hiring keypunch operators and directed me to the human resources department to complete an application. An HR rep invited me into her office, explaining that my daughter would be fine waiting for me in the outer office. I thanked her, but had no intentions of leaving my child alone, so I brought her into the interview with me. She stood quietly beside me for the 15-minute interview. When the rep asked how fast I typed and key punched, I told her I typed 70-plus words a minute, but didn't know how fast I could key punch, since I had never done that. I figured since I could type as fast as I could talk, I could certainly enter numbers with accuracy. By the grace of God, she apparently agreed and didn't delve any further but began explaining where I should park when I returned for work.

My hours were 4 to 11 p.m., not an ideal schedule for a mom with two small children. Yet, the job allowed me to quickly pay off the ministry pledge I had made. Plus, I didn't have to hire a babysitter since my husband worked an early shift and was at home with the children before I left for work. God honored my faith by blessing me with that job, so that I could fulfill the pledge I'd made. But He didn't stop there. Within a few months, he had multiplied the seed into a much better job more closely related to my career path. What surprised me most was the way He pulled it off.

I had only been at the yearbook company for a few months – just long enough to pay off my pledge – when my husband's boss sent him to install phone cable lines for a new NBC News satellite operation in south Charlotte. My husband told NBC's site manager that I was a writer and asked if they needed writers. The guy told him they did and gave him the name and number of the hiring manager. About a month later, they hired me as a national desk scriptwriter. Of all the people they hired, I was the only one in their newsroom who had never worked in television.

Until then, I had been a newspaper reporter. God is so awesome!

My little $100 pledge sure seemed like an insignificant seed going toward a multi-million dollar project. But God not only multiplied the seed, He multiplied my tithes, the 10 percent of my gross income, which goes to my church, and continues to multiply it.

I fell in love with the concept of sowing and reaping a few years earlier after hearing a church member named Ossie Rendleman share a similar testimony. Based on her testimony, I knew it would work for me because it had worked for her. I just didn't know to what degree it would work for me. Ossie was a housewife, who found a job just to finance a building pledge to our ministry. As a result, God increased her income so that she no longer had to shop at bargain stores, but could afford to shop wherever she pleased.

Although I'm not much of a shopper, I was thrilled to learn from her experience just how easy it was to apply the law of sowing and reaping. She seared an image into my spirit I will never forget. Had I mentioned to folks in my old church circle that I was getting a job to contribute to a ministry, they would have thought I had lost my mind. But iron sharpens iron, and I've grown to love being around people whose testimonies and encouraging words strengthen my faith (Proverbs 27:17).

Still, I was fairly new to word of faith teachings, and I wasn't exactly sure how the law of sowing and reaping worked. But I had seen for myself it definitely worked, and I now know sowing and reaping is God's primary method for prospering His people. I was pretty new at discerning God's voice too, since this was the first church I'd ever attended where, not just the pastor, but the members actually studied the Bible on their own time away from church. I realized the more I studied the Bible, the more clearly I could discern God's voice.

One Sunday night, as I was sitting in the back of the sanctuary waiting for our adult Bible study class to begin, the Lord spoke to me, not in an audible voice, but in my spirit and told me to give the lady sitting behind me $7. My initial response was, "She doesn't know me that well, and I'm going to look really foolish handing her just $7." I felt like she would be pretty insulted. But just as class was about to begin, the Lord prompted me again, "Give her $7." I thought, "Lord, why would I do that? I could at least give her $10. If I give her $7, she'll probably say, "If that's all you can spare, you need to keep that for yourself."

But I got no more promptings concerning it. So, I said, "Ok, Lord. I'll do it. You must have a reason." So I reached over and got my purse and pulled out my wallet. When I opened the main bill section, to my surprise, all I found was $7 – one five and two ones. I thought surely I had some money in another compartment, so I began searching through every section looking for it. I didn't remember breaking my last $10, so I knew there had to be some money tucked away somewhere else. But I was wrong. I couldn't find an extra dime. I had exactly $7.

I turned around to see if the lady and her two children were still sitting there, kind of hoping they had moved. But they were just sitting there. Don't get me wrong. I had no qualms about parting with the money; I just didn't want to make a fool of myself. I figured I could at least run to the teller machine and grab $10 or $15 more to give her, and if she had gone home by the time I got back, I could always bring it to church on Wednesday night. But God wasn't impressed with my rebellious spirit of pride, and in my spirit, I knew He would not be satisfied until I did exactly what He was silently prompting me to do. Finally, I leaned back over my chair and quietly said to the lady, "I don't know why, but God told me to give you this $7." She thanked me and quickly took the money out of my hand.

When service ended, and I was heading toward the door, the lady walked over to me and gave me a hug. With tears in her eyes, she said, "You just don't know how much this blessed me. Before we left the house this evening, I told my children that God was our source, not their daddy. I told them God would provide them lunch money for the week. Then you turned around and gave me $7. That's how much I needed to get them lunch for the week."

At that moment I was confident I had heard from God, and I was so glad I obeyed. But I also realized just how self-centered and puffed up with pride I was, so much so that I almost missed an opportunity for God to bless someone through me. I wanted to give her a bigger gift because of the way it would have made me look in her eyes. I hadn't considered the fact that God was well able to multiply any sized gift, and that if He told me to give her a specific amount, He was the one supplying her need, not me. I was simply a vessel. Unfortunately, I wasn't a willing one.

I asked the Lord to forgive me for my attitude and give me more opportunities to bless people. He gave me one opportunity after another. Sometimes I blew it, and sometimes I hit it head on.

First Samuel 15:22 (Amplified) helped me to better understand God's requirement for obedience. Here is the background: When God sent Saul into battle against the Amalekites, God told him to kill every man, woman, infant and child. God also told him to totally destroy all the livestock. But Saul destroyed every weak and lame animal and kept the best livestock for himself. He told the Prophet Samuel his men had spared the cattle to offer as a sacrifice to the Lord as if he had no authority over them. He also kept Agag, the King of Amalek, alive, although God had instructed Saul to kill him. The Prophet Samuel said to Saul, "Has the Lord as great a delight in burnt offerings and sacrifices as in obeying the voice of the Lord? Behold, to obey is better than sacrifice, and to hearken than the fat of rams."

That scripture assured me I had done the right thing by following God's promptings in my spirit. I only began to doubt when I pondered the type of response I would receive. God rarely speaks to everyone at the same time. It's okay for Him to tell me to do something kind for you without ever revealing to you He's teaching me obedience. That part may not pertain to you. I knew that God would continue giving me opportunities to develop in this area.

Some years later, I learned the mother of one of my daughter's classmates was going through a divorce, and since I wasn't close to her, I said nothing to her about it. I didn't want her to think I was prying into her business. But since I had gone through a divorce several years earlier and knew how lonely and inadequate it left me feeling, I began praying for her. The Lord led me to go to the Christian bookstore near my house, purchase a real nice inspirational card, drop two hundred dollars in it and give it to her. I found what I thought was an almost perfectly-worded card with beautiful bright images on front. But what really sold me on this card was the genuineness of the text inside, which simply commended her for being such a wonderful, loving and caring mother. I didn't bother to add a note to it. I just wrote her name at the top and signed mine at the bottom. It was just a thinking-of-you card. Although nothing in its wording indicated that I knew she was going through a divorce, I thought certainly this card would pick her up and cause her to feel God's love for her in spite of what she was going through. I couldn't wait to give it to her the next time I saw her since our children caught the same bus.

"Hi Mary (not her real name), this is for you," I said, handing her the card. She stopped just a few steps away from me, opened it and quickly read it. I turned to walk away, but stopped when I looked up and saw her standing in front of me. She looked pretty perturbed.

"Why did you give me this?" she demanded sternly without cracking a smile.

"Because I felt led of the Lord to sow a seed," I said.

"But why did you give this to me?" she repeated sounding a little more annoyed. Her tone of voice implied she not only was offended, but that she was skeptical of my motive for the gift.

I said, "Because I heard you were going through a divorce, and I felt led to give you a card to encourage you."

"Oh," she said without ever changing her facial expression. Then she walked away without saying thanks, or anything. But in spite of her response, this time I knew I had done exactly what the Lord had placed in my heart.

I believe the Lord was just reaffirming to me that even when He gives me instructions that appear illogical, not to look for people's approval. He was trying to strengthen my faith in Him and break a negative trait that had plagued me all my life. There was a time when I would have retorted just as abruptly as that lady with, "Honey, if you can't use $200, just give me my money back." But I knew I hadn't missed God.

Having been in her shoes, I knew she was just responding out of hurt and embarrassment. She simply didn't know how to receive such a personal gift from someone she hardly knew. Had I become offended and taken it personally, I would have hindered God's outpouring of love to her through me and stopped the blessings He had planned to multiply back to me from the seed He told me to sow. About 10 years later, that same lady stopped me and told me she couldn't remember ever thanking me for the card. She also told me how much she appreciated it.

God had shown me that love demands unconditional giving that is not driven by feelings or emotions. That's because love is a seed, not an emotion. Somehow I knew it wasn't the end of the lesson either, and I was right. As God began placing more demands on my finances, He increased my income to meet those demands. As part of that lesson, I began to sense His urging to give more to individuals and ministries spreading the gospel. I learned not to give out of emotion, especially to ministries with tear-jerking pleas for money to feed the hungry, help save their ministries or prevent their broadcasts from going off the air.

As a steward of God's resources, I knew I had to pray before writing a check out or making a commitment to help finance food and clothing for people in third world countries. While every televised outreach was appealing, not all of them appropriated finances in the manner alluded to in their TV ads. God showed me over and over that I was blessed to be a blessing to others, which requires fiscal accountability and rock solid stewardship.

Not only did God take me out of my comfort zone in giving, He led me to support projects I wouldn't have ever gotten involved with, not in my wildest dreams. One of them was an aviation outreach that I had never even heard of. It flew sick and dying people from devastated areas and impoverished countries all over the globe to medical centers for emergency treatment. Another outreach God laid on my heart to support finances flights for Jewish people relocating to Israel. Heightened anti-Semitism creates deplorable substandard living conditions in many countries, forcing Jews in the former Soviet Union, Ethiopia and other parts of Africa and Europe to flee for their lives to a safe haven in Israel. Before, I couldn't imagine myself pouring money into anything not related to helping impoverished third-world children. But I did, along with other international outreaches; and God always sees to it I reap a harvest.

When the major bank I worked for phased out my department and laid me off, the financial seeds I had sown in various ministries were multiplied back to me several times over. I didn't want for anything. I actually wound up with a lot more money in my bank account while unemployed than I had ever had while working. I never panicked over being unemployed because I knew God had my back. There's a saying, "If you're about His business, He'll be about yours." I honestly believe that, and I would tell anyone who inquired about my job options that I would have a new job within a few months. I had worked as a communications specialist for the bank's retail mortgage division. Coming out of such a stressful, high-profile position, I actually looked forward to having a few months off to relax and un-stress. All my bills were paid on time or ahead of time, so I saw it as God blessing me with a paid two-month vacation.

Within months, I was resolving delinquent accounts for a huge financial conglomerate where I eventually moved into mortgage and personal loan sales. Through these roles I learned many of the financial industry's tricks of the trade and debt trap schemes. It wasn't long before I became a perpetrator, placing debt's noose around the necks of many innocent victims. As they struggled to break free from its daunting grip, many clung for dear life to their peace, health and financial stability.

The next chapter deals with some of the industry's most popular scams. These schemes, which are usually marketed as legitimate business arrangements, appear credible because they're spotlighted in sensational primetime television commercials and innocently touted through word of mouth by friends and relatives. After all, it's a lot easier for us to trust the recommendations of people we know.

Chapter 8
Beware of Schemes & Scams

Several perfectly legal marketing schemes have been devised especially for people who appear to lack financial savvy. Among them are enterprises that market rent-to-own houses, rent-to-own furniture, prepaid legal services and payday loans. Rent-to-own companies typically target customers who struggle with money management, poor credit ratings, multiple charged-off accounts and some repos. It's the type of customer most reputable establishments hate to see coming. They're the ones who have never paid anyone on time for anything. Yet they're prime targets for business predators because they rarely research the actual costs of what they're renting. Therefore, they're willing to pay just about anything as long as it's broken into low easy-to-manage payments.

Rent-to-own landlords capitalize on this type of customer by charging them anywhere from three to five times what the property is worth. For example, the owner of a house with a $600 monthly mortgage would charge at least $1,800 a month to a rent-to-own customer. That way even if the client defaults after six months, the homeowner would have netted $7,200 in profits from monthly rental plus a non-refundable deposit. Because these renters have to pay a hefty deposit up front, homeowners often make more money from renters who default than from those who fulfill long-term rental commitments. These deposits or "down payments" are often nonrefundable, or refunded solely at the owner's discretion.

Some contracts are worded to imply the deposit would be deducted from the total sale price of the house. Yet, these contracts often include some type of trial rental period, as if homeowners are grading renters to determine if they are worthy of homeownership. Whether the property actually changes hands at the end of the trial is solely at the owner's discretion. If you earned a fortune renting property for two to three times the value, what would motivate you to sell it? Since renters receive no tax credit for rent-to-own homes, a lot of times, they are better off renting an apartment until they come across a better deal.

You could save tons of money by purchasing a house on your own, especially a short sale or foreclosed property. There are several private, non-profit and government-backed programs to help first-time homeowners. Some offer credit counseling for those with marred credit, as well as low interest rates and subsidies for down payments.

Rent-to-own furniture stores target the same clientele and operate similar to those offering rent-to-own houses. Their customers don't think twice about paying $85 a month to rent a laptop valued at $300 stretched out over a two-year contract. With the exception of corporate clients, most rent-to-own patrons are those with no credit or bad credit. If renters held onto a basic laptop for the life of the contract, they could wind up paying several times its value.

When my son and a few of his college friends moved into their first apartment off campus, I couldn't convince him that buying used furniture was far more practical than renting it. He blew me off as if what I said had come straight out of the Civil War Antebellum Era. No matter how well I explained it, I think what he heard was: "Go west, young man, and there you'll find your 40 acres and a mule."

"Rent to own is what college people do now days, Mama," he said. Besides, they had found a heck-of-a "deal," a complete room of furniture, including end tables for only $80 a month. So I just left it alone. They all worked part-time jobs, but none had taken into consideration how they would foot the bill, along with rent, electricity, cable, food and entertainment, if one of them moved out or lost his job. When faced with eviction notices, it occurred to them that they might have been living a little above their means. But it was a lesson that sunk in too late, and I offered no money or advice toward a bail out.

Payday loan establishments are equivalent to modern-day loan sharks. At one time, they were banned from North

Carolina because they're such a rip-off. Unfortunately, that didn't stop cash-strapped consumers from driving across state lines to borrow from them. But they're back! They target clients who struggle to manage money between paydays, charging as much as 50 percent interest. Customers in search of a one-time quick fix find themselves addicted and indebted to them for years because of the astronomical interest and fees charged.

Run from Settlement Services

Settlement companies are another scam you should avoid like the plague. They target people who are too stressed out to think straight. Their best clients are those under tremendous pressure from creditors due to missed payments. These operations, typically run by attorneys, offer to settle your debts for a monthly charge. They charge clients a percentage of their debts while advising them not to pay creditors. Clients often assume these firms are negotiating with creditors on their behalf. But instead, the attorneys are simply holding their clients' money in interest-bearing accounts for four months to wait for the debts to charge off. Once an account charges off, the attorney contacts the creditor and offers to pay a settlement, or fraction of the balance owed.

Because the settlement business has become so lucrative for attorneys, many cash-strapped clients seeking bankruptcy advice are being routed toward settlements instead. Clients rarely understand what's involved in the settlement services offered. But anyone can stop paying creditors for four months, let the accounts charge off and then call and offer to pay a percentage of the balance. So why pay an attorney to do that? Accounts charge off all by themselves for free. If you're unsure of the settlement percentages to offer, just sit tight and your creditors will contact you with a settlement offer.

Prepaid legal services are another pretty poor investment for those of us who work hard for our money. This product is especially designed for those who are looking for something for nothing. Unless you're planning to search for opportunities to sue people, this is a total waste of money. Why would anybody pay monthly legal fees just in case they're involved in a skirmish that merits a lawsuit? Besides, these services don't cover attorney fees, but offer consumers a discount on legal services rendered. It's such an iffy proposition you'd be better off bypassing them and placing your money in a CD or other interest-bearing account. Pre-paid legal is a game of chance that's about as uncertain as winning the lottery. It implies that if you just keep paying $25 a month, eventually you'll luck up on a lawsuit worth millions that's going to set you up for life. Pure BULL!

It reminds me of a time when I was driving back to Charlotte from Hampton Roads and stopped at a convenience store to fill up my car. When I got to the checkout counter, an older woman was paying for her items. She stopped to send two small children back to the car. After paying, she handed the clerk a large pack of chewing gum, which I assumed she had forgotten to give him.

"That'll be $1.77," he said after ringing up the gum.

"One-seventy-seven," she screamed. "You got to be kidding. I'm not paying a dollar and seventy-seven cents for a pack of gum. I could see a dollar, but not a dollar and seventy-seven cents."

She stood silently staring at the clerk, who looked at her and chuckled to himself. It was a standoff. Nobody was saying anything. I started to pay the seventy-seven cent difference, since I had a four-hour drive ahead of me and wanted to get home before dark.

"This is for the children," she said as if pleading for some great humanitarian cause. "I'm buying this for the children," she repeated cutting her eyes back at me.

I thought, "What theatrics. Something's wrong with this picture." It wasn't any of the typical children's brands. I didn't know of any young children who preferred breath-freshening gum. So rather than intervene, I decided to just observe. After a few more seconds of silence, she slapped the gum on the counter, snarling, "I'm not paying for this," and stormed out of the store. Kind of confused about what had transpired, I asked the clerk if she expected him to discount the gum.

Still chuckling, he replied while pointing to a machine on the back wall: "I don't know. Maybe so, but she just spent $40 on the lottery."

Unnecessary Auto Totaling

If your car is involved in the slightest fender bender, drivers, BEWARE! At the drop of a hat some insurance companies will total your vehicle unnecessarily to avoid paying for the most minor repairs. They'll cut you a check based on the vehicle's used car market value and then resell it wholesale at an auction. Since cars depreciate as soon as they're driven off the lot, oftentimes, the check isn't enough to replace the vehicle with one of equal value.

To discourage drivers from using insurance to get their cars fixed, adjusters may exaggerate the cost of repairs, which they substantiate with tale's about the vehicle's frame being so badly bent it could never function properly. These knee-jerk assessments may be delivered with such authority many car owners assume their only choice is totaling their vehicles. But it's not. Regardless of the repair cost, it's your right as the vehicle owner, not that of the insurance company, to decide if your vehicle is totaled or repaired. I know several people who were told their vehicles had to be totaled following minor accidents.

As a matter of fact, I was told the same thing after I rammed into the side of a passenger van, tearing off my entire front bumper and part of my hood. I told the adjuster, "Absolutely not! You will NOT total my car," and that was the end of that. The insurance company paid to have it fixed, and five years later with over 200,000 miles, it drives just fine. One clue that an insurance company is lying to you about the cost of repairs is when the person assessing your damage, generally wearing a shirt and tie, knows absolutely nothing about auto mechanics. Another tell-tale sign is when you're given a huge repair estimate before your car is ever placed on a rack or hooked up to diagnostic equipment.

On the bright side, here's how you can turn your minor car accident into a profitable venture. When you realize the other guy's insurance company has given you a ridiculously pricey quote to repair your vehicle, but is offering you a handsome check to total it, simply accept the check if it's much more than enough to cover actual repairs. But first find out from the insurance folks when and where your car will be auctioned, so you can show up and buy it back at wholesale price. After spending a fraction of the insurance check to buy your vehicle back, have your own mechanic fix it for next to nothing. Nearly all totaled vehicles wind up at auctions, but occasionally, some land in the hands of other third parties. So don't assume your car's going to auction, because it could be earmarked for an agent's relative or friend. Ask where your car's headed before accepting a dime. Some insurance companies will allow you to buy it back at wholesale price before it ever reaches the auction block.

Odometer Misreading Errors

Another costly mistake we make is failing to carefully review our receipts after having auto repairs and parts replaced under warranty. It's not uncommon for sales and repair shops to record erroneous odometer readings. Let's say you purchased new tires or batteries with warranties that are good for five years or 60,000 miles. Instead of listing the car's actual mileage, shop attendants sometimes note accounts as showing thousands of miles less than the odometer.

If you fail to notice this, when you return demanding replacements under the warranty, all records will show you're not eligible because you've exceeded the mileage requirement. Ladies especially should beware! That happened to me twice that I'm aware of. The receipt for my tires was short 40,000 miles, and my battery receipt was short 50,000 miles. Because I caught it in time, the shops reprinted them with the correct mileage.

God's Divine Order Leads to Prosperity – Confusion Leads to Lack

God is a God of order. Everything He does has a plan. He didn't just slap a few stars in the sky and create the sun and moon before realizing He hadn't finished arranging the stars. He created the entire universe with purpose and precision. Likewise, He expects us to manage our finances in an orderly fashion.

A major key to getting our finances in order is prioritizing bills based on their importance. When our finances are tight and we place our necessities above our wants, we're demonstrating to God our discipline. Necessities are those things that are essential to your health and wellbeing. Wants are those things that make life more comfortable, but we can really live without.

When bill collectors turn up the heat, calling two or three times a day, it's better to let the answering machine pick up if you're unable to tell them the date you will pay. That way you don't feel coerced into lying to get them off the phone. Plus you avoid the pressure of postdating debits or checks that could cause more important obligations to bounce.

Below is a sample list of bills by priority.

1) Mortgage or rent
2) Childcare (if you've got a job)
3) Electricity
4) Natural gas
5) Auto or transportation to work
6) Water
7) Primary phone
8) Loans and credit cards
9) Groceries
10) Secondary phone(s)
11) Entertainment – cable or satellite TV& internet

Paying creditors in order of importance shows we have integrity. It not only removes guilt, it also gives us the confidence to boldly ask God to intervene when we command financial obstacles to move (Mark 11:22-23). It's difficult to go to God boldly requesting money to catch up a car payment if you've just made a huge down payment on a cruise. Especially in a crunch, being in the habit of paying the mortgage ahead of the utilities could keep you in your house. So many houses go into foreclosure with the electricity, gas, water and cable still turned on. Since those aren't amenities one can enjoy looking through the window from outside, paying them ahead of the mortgage simply reflects misaligned priorities.

Chapter 9
Faith Only Works by Love

As Christians we have been commanded by God to bring tithes into His storehouse, which is the church or wherever we are fed spiritually. While everything we have belongs to God, He only requires us to give Him back 10 percent of our gross income. When we withhold our tithes, we rob God and subject our lives to the curse of poverty, according to Malachi 3:8-9. The tithe is 10 percent of our income, not our time or service, since there's no way of honestly measuring those.

By bringing our tithes, we demonstrate our love for God and our faith and trust in Him. When we resort to other means to finance the gospel, we're demonstrating our lack of trust in God's integrity. Without faith, it's impossible to please God, but faith only works by love (Hebrews 11:6 and Galatians 5:6). I've never had a problem with tithing, even when I didn't understand how it worked.

My challenge, over the years, has been with walking in love. I have approached God with a totally condemning attitude about others and felt pretty justified about it, especially if someone had offended me. At one time, I had two neighbors who cared for foster children. One, I considered a model parent. She kept the two little boys in her care immaculate. Their clothes were neatly pressed and color coordinated, their faces always clean and their hair always looked freshly cut and trimmed. She was always immaculate too.

The other foster parent was just the opposite. She kept a little boy and girl, whose clothes were always dirty and raggedy, and their shoes were worn out and full of holes. Their hair was dirty, matted and oily, and the children literally scratched like dogs.

Her appearance had improved immensely since she had taken them in. She bought a new wardrobe and began going to the beauty salon regularly. But what I found disgusting was the fact the two children in her care looked totally unkempt. I thought, "Dear Lord, how ridiculously unkind of her to not take any better care of those children." I felt sorry for them and anger toward her because I felt she was neglecting them.

When I pointed this horrible situation out to the Lord, I was quite surprised by His response. All He said was: "You can bless them with new clothes and shoes." I thought, "Why in the world should I buy clothes and shoes for them when she's squandering the money she's receiving for that purpose?" It looked like she was spending all the money she received to care for them on herself.

Based on my limited assessment of the situation, I decided not to give the children anything. I thought this foster mother really didn't deserve any help from anybody because, at least in my eyes, she was just being selfish. Shortly afterward, the children were moved somewhere else, and I never got confirmation one way or another.

But what if God thought like I had and only blessed us when He felt we really deserved it? Most of us, especially me, wouldn't be here to read this. In spite of our selfishness and reckless lifestyles, He sent His only son to die for our sins and to make us heirs to His abundant mercy and grace, not because mankind deserved it but because of His unconditional love for us. Now who was I to condemn this woman to the point that I wouldn't reach out to help two very needy children in her care?

Some of the greatest blessings I've experienced in my life have come when I've done something above and beyond the call of duty, just out of love for someone I felt really didn't deserve it. When I worked with a team of case managers for county government, there was a guy on our team whose poor work ethic severely hurt production for our whole team. He would set out in the mornings heading to visit clients and often wouldn't return to work until the next day.

Case managers were required to document their client interventions daily, so the state could compensate our agency for the work. But this guy always waited until the end of the month to document his all at once. By then, he either couldn't remember the details since most were made up, or just didn't feel like inputting the notes.

When he was out of town for a family emergency, I called to check on him and asked if I could input his notes. By the time he returned to work, I had completely caught him up, and I continued entering them so he wouldn't become overwhelmed again. As a result, he went from being the lowest producer on the team to the top performer. Even the department head commended me for jumping in and taking on the additional responsibility, which boosted the team's production to first place.

My teammate also thanked me and apologized for not being motivated to carry his load. He was disenchanted with the job because it offered no room to grow. Empathizing with him, I explained that I had a degree in journalism and background in communications and how I longed to return to my field. He told me his wife, an executive at a major bank, was looking for someone with my background and asked for my resume to pass on. Within a few weeks, I got a call from the human resources department at his wife's bank, inviting me for an interview. Within a month, I was hired as an assistant vice president in corporate communications with a great starting salary and a month's vacation.

Wow! God had taken my simple costless seed of kindness and turned it into an avalanche of blessings. All I did was input case management notes for a teammate, and God used that seed to open the door to the best paying job I'd ever had. That's just God's nature. Whenever He tells me to sow a seed of kindness that may seem absolutely ridiculous, and I obey, He always blesses me with a ridiculous harvest in return. Even when I've let go of bitterness and strife toward folks I wasn't fond of and shown them kindness, God has seen to it that I experienced an immediate outpouring of His love and generosity.

Chapter 10
What's in Your House?

Fear of failure had been my most stifling hurdle, and it prevented me from going after my dreams. I'd find myself procrastinating over measures I could have easily taken to accomplish my goals. But paralyzing fear was at the root of my procrastination.

At times, procrastination caused me to feel like an absolute failure because I wasn't moving forward toward accomplishing anything. It seemed my life was at a standstill when in actuality, there's no such thing as a standstill. You're either moving forward toward a dream or moving backward away from it. The fact that I was actually moving backward was a reality I wasn't prepared to deal with. I would think about people who could barely read and write; yet, they managed to write two or three books. My excuse for neglecting work on my own book was I was too busy editing and publishing books for other people, as if I couldn't do both – write books and publish, like chew gum and walk.

The frustration for me was in realizing these folks were confident enough in their talents to use whatever writing skills they had. Yet, for years, I had been sitting on my talents and skills coming up with one excuse after another as to why I wasn't using them. On several occasions, I heard messages with scriptures encouraging me on this very topic. I took the time to boldly highlight those scriptures in my Bible, so they would stand out when I wanted to meditate on them, but for years, I failed to act on them. Yet, I knew God had placed them in my heart to do. I knew there was a message in Isaiah 54: 2-4 specifically for me, although when the Prophet Isaiah wrote this, thousands of years ago, he was addressing the children of Israel:

"Enlarge the place of your tent,
And let them stretch out the curtains of your dwellings;
Do not spare;
Lengthen your cords,
And strengthen your stakes.
For you shall expand to the right and to the left...
Do not fear, for you will not be ashamed..."

In this passage, God is telling us to go for it. Just do it. Regardless of the hindrances, in spite of the obstacles, just step out on faith, and He'll cause circumstances to materialize for us that are beyond our wildest imaginations. But we can't get to that point if we allow fear to stagnate us. Fear moves us away from faith and away from pursuing the dreams God has given us. When consumed by fear, we rely on gaining favor with people we think can help us achieve our goals. That mindset embedded in the world's system is based on the philosophy, "If you scratch my back, I'll scratch yours."

Unfortunately, there's no integrity in it because those operating under its influence can be bought, swayed and frightened into making decisions that affect you. But God is a God of integrity and unconditional love. He can't be bought, influenced or blindsided by those with ulterior motives. Likewise, He has no fear of anything or anybody because He created everything and everybody. He responds solely to our faith, which according to Galatians 5:6, works by love.

The Message Bible puts it this way: *"For in Christ, neither our most conscientious religion nor disregard of religion amounts to anything. What matters is something far more interior: faith expressed in love."*

This scripture explains why we must activate our faith through love in order for God to move on our behalf. Bitterness and strife turn our focus backward. I heard a college dean put it this way: "God can only bless a forward-moving vessel." We are the vessels. When we move forward toward our dreams and goals, rather than allow offenses to sidetrack us, we demonstrate our faith in Him.

God's not expecting us to accomplish great feats all by ourselves. But He does want to prosper mankind through us, using the talents and skills He's given us. And He wants to do it using what we've already got. Often times, no costly preparation is required. He's simply asking us, "What's in your house?"

On numerous occasions, I've overlooked resources right at my fingertips in my own house, wishing I had more money to spend on projects. At one point, I thought, "If I only had the money to pay somebody to create a really slick website for me, I could really get my business off the ground." Yet, just eight years prior, I built a website for a small business owner, using free online tools. I not only thoroughly enjoyed building the site, but the guy paid me to do it. What altered my attitude so drastically that my image of myself changed from provider to consumer over an eight-year period? Unconsciously, I allowed a spirit of fear to set in, which caused complacency and procrastination to push me backward and stifle my creativity.

That attitude grows like wild fire when I make excuses to pacify myself. It says, "Just let somebody else do it." But why would I pay to have someone create a site I could easily develop myself? The cost of hiring someone should have been the deciding factor, but it wasn't. Somehow I had completely forgotten I had those skills.

I had known for years that God was trying to take me to a new level – spiritually, mentally and physically. But at times, I felt I wasn't seeing any progress and just beating my head against a wall in frustration. It hadn't occurred to me that I was the one steering the ship. And unless I started steering it toward my goal, I wasn't going to move, at least not in the direction I wanted to go. Few people stumble across success while just chilling. It's birthed out of trial and error for those who refuse to give up. Even for those who inherit instant success, hard work is required to hold onto it.

Like me, many people have sacrificed and prepared all their lives to make the companies they work for successful. You've probably also donated countless hours helping friends and associates fulfill their visions. I'll never stop giving to others because giving is an outpouring of love that brings me joy and satisfaction. But sometimes I feel like I've sown enough seed to harvest a crop the size of China.

To achieve my goals in life, I realized I had to safeguard my priorities by jumping off of that constantly busy treadmill where others bogarted my time and skills with never-ending "good" deeds. Trying to talk our way out of invitations can be demeaning and pointless, especially when all it takes is saying "No." This two-letter word has been my best strategy for staying focused. It helps me deal with persistent people who try to back me into a corner, as well as manipulative ones who shower me with kindness expecting favors in return.

Here are three tactful, guilt-free ways I've learned to say "no" to unwanted offers and invitations:

- "No."
- "I wish I could, but no, I won't be able to."
- "Let me get back to you on that."

After responding, I've learned to change the subject or end the conversation without offering any explanation. Try it. It's addictive. But the best part about it is it eliminates pressure. Mounting pressure leads to strife, which causes sickness -- a major debt trap. When I've yielded to manipulation and gone places or assisted with projects that weren't convenient, sometimes, I've felt frustrated and resentful afterward. Now, I simply say "no."

This unclutters my schedule, giving me more quiet time to talk with God and meditate on His instructions to me. Eliminating distractions puts me at peace and allows my imagination to roam. That's how I came to realize God had already placed within my house every tool needed to win. Just like me, He's given you dreams and desires, compassion, talents, skills and the mind of Christ. It's up to us whether we use them or ignore them.

One Old Testament widow was desperate enough to use what little she had. Unable to pay her bills, she pleaded with Elisha to stop her creditor from taking her sons away as slaves (2 Kings 4:1-7). When Elisha asked what was in her house, she replied nothing but a jar of oil. He advised her to borrow as many empty vessels from neighbors as she could. He was enlarging her vision, preparing her mentally to receive, not just enough to get by, but enough to live on forever. Then he gave her specific instructions on what to do with the jar of oil once she got the empty vessels home.

"And when you have come in, you shall shut the door behind you and your sons; then pour it into all those vessels, and set aside the full ones."

Elisha multiplied the oil in her jar, so that it filled each vessel. Once she ran out of vessels, the oil stopped multiplying. Elisha then told her to sell the oil, pay her debt and use the money for her and her sons to live.

As a result of her obedience and gratitude for the one asset she owned, she was financially set for the rest of her life. The best part of the story is she didn't have to invest one dime to get it. The jar of oil was already in her house. The vessels were from neighbors who probably knew her and her family, and some may have been relatives. The word *borrow* implies she had to return the vessels to their owners at some point or replace them with an equivalent vessel or service. But when she gave them back, she didn't have to pay interest on them, nor had she signed over her house as collateral.

By pointing out the oil, she was showing gratitude for her only asset. Had she totally disregarded it as insignificant, she wouldn't have mentioned it, releasing faith-filled words as seed for God to multiply. Remember, the prophet never came into her house to look for valuables, but asked her what she owned.

Had she thought like some Christians, she may have argued with the prophet about the history of that oil, where it came from, how long she had owned it, why she hadn't used it and why no one would buy it from her in that economy. Instead she acted on the prophet's instructions by faith.

Many times, I missed the most crucial step by failing to act on instructions. I would receive the inspired word with excitement and joy and even make a few faith confessions based on messages I had heard.

It was as if I thought confessing something enough would suddenly cause it to magically appear. Actually, that's about as effective as sitting home after losing a job and confessing, "Money comes to me. Money comes to me," but never taking steps to acquire new income.

I'm not knocking the power of faith confessions or positive words because unless we speak our visions (whatever we're hoping for), they'll never come to pass. Faith is the substance of things hoped for and the evidence of things not seen (Hebrews 11:1). When we stop talking about our visions, we lose hope and they die. Just mentioning them periodically to someone we trust helps keep them within reach and in the forefront of our minds.

Whenever God has reminded me of what's in my house, He was prompting me to step out of my comfort zone. I believe God has given each of us talents in specific areas, expecting our gifts to open doors to prosper us (Proverbs 18:16). I realized as early as adolescence that what motivated me most was writing. I never aspired to become a banker, a salesperson, or anything unrelated to writing. For years, I neglected my real interests so that I could stay in the workforce shuffle where most people are stuck, just existing to pay bills. But not anymore! I'm convinced that if you pursue God's vision for your life, determined to use your gifts and talents, you are destined to prosper.

If debt has prevented you from achieving your goals and fulfilling your vision, now's the time to move forward. To accelerate we must stop borrowing, downsize when necessary, maintain priorities and avoid marketing schemes. As you step out on faith, talking like God has already given you the victory, make sure you're walking in love and planting financial seeds into good ground, and

He'll work behind the scenes to quickly bring it to pass. But first, make sure your relationship with Christ is intact.

If you're out of fellowship with God, you can make Him the center of your life by praying the following prayer out loud and meaning it from your heart:

Dear Lord,

I come to you just as I am. You know my life. You know how I've lived. Forgive me Lord. I repent of my sins. I believe Jesus Christ is the Son of God. He died for my sins, and on the third day, He arose from the dead. Lord Jesus, I ask you to come into my heart and live your life in me and through me from now on. From this day forward, I belong to you, in Jesus' name. Amen.

Your next important step is to speak powerful faith-filled words over your finances daily. Here are some great confessions to make:

1. Wealth and riches are in my house (Psalm 112:3).

2. God gives me power to get wealth (Deuteronomy 8:18).

3. The blessing of the Lord makes me rich, and He adds no sorrow with it (Proverbs 10:22).

4. Because I am a tither, the windows of heaven are open to me and the devourer is rebuked for my sake (Malachi 3:10-11).

5. I'm blessed in the city and in the field, coming and going, in business ventures and in my family life. Everything I put my hand to is blessed (Deuteronomy 28:2-6).

6. I will lend, but I will not borrow (Deuteronomy 28:12).

7. I owe no man anything but love (Romans 13:8).

8. My steps are ordered by the Lord (Psalm 37:23). A stranger I won't follow (John 10:5).

9. I have everything that pertains to life and godliness (2 Peter 1:3).

10. I'm blessed to be a blessing (Genesis 12:2).

11. God's grace abounds toward me, giving me abundance for every good work (2 Corinthians 9:8).

12. When the enemy comes against me, like a flood the Spirit of the Lord will lift up a standard against him (Isaiah 59:19).

13. No weapon formed against me shall prosper (Isaiah 54:17).

14. I can do all things through Christ who strengthens me (Philippians 4:13).

15. The Lord teaches me to profit and leads me in the way I should go (Isaiah 48:17).

16. My gifts make room for me and bring me before great men (Proverbs 18:16).

Praise God! You've just been empowered to win and to win big. Now activate your faith by applying what you've learned. Be sure to thank God daily for bringing you out of debt and for causing the vision He placed in your heart to flourish and succeed. I rejoice with you, knowing that it's already done. As you move forward, may God's richest and best blessings overtake you!